PCs made easy

A PRACTICAL COURSE

STAGE 1

PCs made easy

A PRACTICAL COURSE

STAGE 1

Reader's Digest

THE READER'S DIGEST ASSOCIATION, INC.
PLEASANTVILLE, NEW YORK / MONTREAL

PCS MADE EASY
A PRACTICAL COURSE – STAGE 1

Published by the Reader's Digest Association, Inc., 2002,
by arrangement with De Agostini UK Ltd

Reader's Digest and the Pegasus logo are registered trademarks
of The Reader's Digest Association, Inc.

READER'S DIGEST PROJECT STAFF
Senior Editor: Don Earnest
Designer: Jennifer R. Tokarski
Production Technology Manager: Douglas A. Croll
Contributing Copyeditor: Nancy Humes

READER'S DIGEST HOME DIVISION
Editorial Director: Christopher Cavanaugh
Art Director: Joan Mazzeo
Marketing Director: Dawn Nelson
Vice President and General Manager: Kiera Kuhs

THE READER'S DIGEST ASSOCIATION, INC
Editor-in-Chief: Eric W. Schrier
President, North America Books and Home Entertainment:
Thomas D. Gardner

PCs made easy was created and produced for
The Reader's Digest Association, Inc. by De Agostini UK Ltd,
from material originally published by De Agostini UK Ltd,
in the UK in periodical form as *Computer Success Plus*.

Copyright © 2000, 2002 De Agostini UK Ltd

Front cover center photograph: Gerhard Steiner, The Stock Market

Library of Congress Cataloging in Publication Data

PCs made easy : a practical course.
    p. cm.
    Contents: [1] Stage one
    ISBN 0-7621-0332-9 (v.1)
            1. Microcomputers. 2. Computer software.

    QA76.5 .P3675 2001
    004.16—dc21
                                                00-045880

Address any comments about *PCs made easy* to:
Editorial Director, Reader's Digest Home Division,
Reader's Digest Road, Pleasantville, NY 10570-7000

To order additional copies of *PCs made easy*, call 1-800-846-2100.

You can also visit us on the World Wide Web at **rd.com**

Printed in the United States of America

CONTENTS

Windows

Starting in Windows

Do you wonder how some people can make their computer work like magic? Do you want to know their secret? Well, it's probably because they know how to use Windows properly. In this section, you will learn the first steps to becoming a Windows wizard.

Without Windows your computer would be nothing but lifeless hardware. Windows operates your PC – which is why it is called an operating system.

Have you noticed how you have to wait for Windows to start before you can begin working with your computer? Once it has started, you can run other software to draw, write or do whatever you want to do. But Windows is always running in the background to help your other programs communicate with your hardware.

You might wonder where Windows got its name. Simple: everything in Windows takes place in its own self-contained window displayed on the screen. You can have many windows on screen at the same time and switch between them. One window might be a word processor, another a painting program or a view of files on your hard disk.

Switch on your PC and the first thing that happens is that Windows loads. Your PC can then run programs that use Windows for essential but basic tasks, such as storing your files and displaying information on screen.

WINDOWS STORY

There have been several versions of Windows. Windows 98 works very much in the same way as the earlier Windows 95. Before that, Windows 3.1 added the graphical interface to the original text-based operating system, MS-DOS.

● **You're in control**

Controlling your computer is easy thanks to the graphical features of Windows. It uses icons (tiny pictures displayed on the screen) to represent different pieces of information, such as letters, pictures and programs. You use a mouse to control Windows, moving your files around, starting programs and so on. Most Windows programs use the same types of commands, which means that many new programs are easy to use because they operate with exactly the same actions and procedures. Learn the basics of Windows and you can control almost any software.

Your Desktop workspace

The first thing you will see after your PC starts up is the Desktop. Think of the Desktop as a self-contained office. It contains a filing cabinet, wastebasket, clock, a menu for starting programs and a way of sending messages to the outside world via the Internet.

My Computer

This lets you browse the files stored on your PC. Move the mouse pointer over this icon and double-click the left mouse button: a new window shows your hard disk, floppy disk and CD-ROM drive, as well as special Printer and Control Panel folders (we'll cover these later in the course).

Network Neighborhood

For office PCs, this lets users see other computers connected to the PC. Most home PC users will not need to use this icon.

Background

The background of the Desktop can be a solid color, a pattern or even a picture. Most new PCs have a solid green-blue background, and some may show the logo of your PC maker.

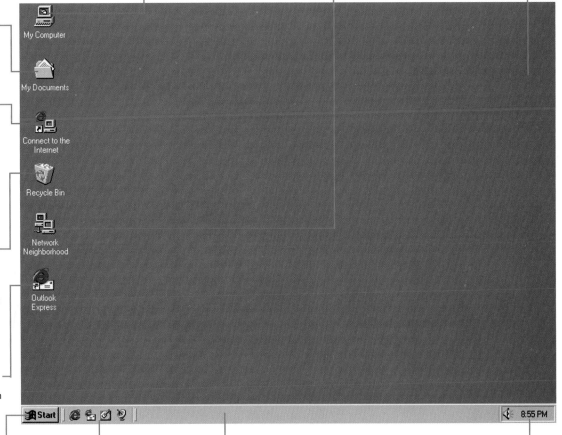

My Documents

This is a shortcut to a ready-made folder on your computer's hard disk.

The Internet

The Internet Connection Wizard is a special program that helps you get on the Internet. You may also have icons for the other Internet services you can subscribe to.

Recycle Bin

When you delete files they go here, so you can easily retrieve them if you make a mistake. To delete the files permanently, you can empty the Recycle Bin.

Outlook Express

This starts Windows' built-in electronic mail program (if you have Internet access).

Start

This button is the main starting point for most of your actions. Click once and you'll see a list of programs and your most recently used documents.

Taskbar buttons

These four buttons let you quickly carry out common tasks, such as connecting to the Internet and minimizing all windows to see the Desktop.

Taskbar

The Taskbar shows you the programs that you are currently running and the windows you have open. To switch between different windows, click on their buttons on the Taskbar.

Status/Time box

This box normally displays the current time, but it can also display other information. Hold the mouse pointer over the time for a moment and a pop-up box tells you the date. The box is also used very often by programs to show the status of tools such as the printer, modem or battery power (on a portable computer).

Starting programs

There are several ways to start a program, but the best is by using the Start button. We shall explain how to use the Start button and look through its pop-up menus to find the programs you want to run. Here's your step-by-step guide.

THE START button is the way you can reach the programs installed on your computer. You'll see this button in the bottom left-hand corner of a gray strip running along the bottom of the screen, called the Taskbar.

The Start button is a real mine of information, containing a list of all the programs and tools that are installed on your PC and storing a list of the last documents that you worked on. Later, we'll show you how to use the other tools that you can see in this menu. There are tools that provide help on any feature of Windows, search for files and set up your PC.

1 Windows' most important button is the Start button at the bottom left of your screen. When you start your PC, you get a helpful reminder of what to do.

2 Click on the Start button and a pop-up menu appears.

3 As you move your mouse up the menu, a colored bar appears on each entry. The small black arrowheads show folders with more items inside. Move the mouse over Programs and a submenu appears.

4 The new list of items contains more options: folders and programs (you might have a few more or less depending on the software you have). The program we want to start is in the Accessories folder. Move the mouse over the Accessories entry and a new submenu appears.

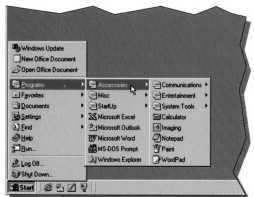

5 Now move the mouse pointer down the list of the items to the entry called Notepad (it also has a small picture – called an icon – that represents a shorthand notebook). Click once with the left mouse button to start the program.

6 As soon as you release the mouse button, Windows finds the Notepad program on your hard disk and starts it up, ready for you to start typing.

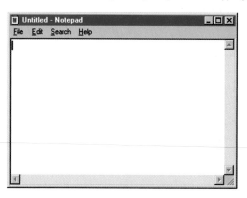

S H O R T C U T

If you want to know more about a command or how to do something in Windows, there's always help available. Just press the [F1] key and a help screen is displayed.

PC TIPS

Tame your mouse

If you find it difficult to click on a menu option, you are probably moving the mouse too fast. Try to relax, and move the mouse slowly and smoothly. If you really can't get the hang of the mouse, then why not cheat for the moment until you are more confident with it: click the Start button with the mouse pointer or, if you have a newer keyboard, press the Start key (in the bottom left corner between the [Ctrl] and [Alt] keys). Now use the arrow keys on the keyboard to move around the menus. Press the [Enter] key to select a menu option.

Moving and resizing windows

Let's learn how to control a Windows program. Since almost all Windows programs have the same standard set of basic commands, once you have mastered Notepad you will be in control and ready to tackle any other program.

1 If you followed the steps on the opposite page, you'll see that the Notepad program is displayed in its own window. The small flashing vertical bar – called the insertion point or text cursor – shows you where your typing will appear.

2 Start by typing names and addresses of friends. As you type, the information fills the window and some moves 'off' the top – just continue typing and Notepad will keep all your text. You can move around the text by using the up and down arrow keys.

3 A quick way to look around your document is to use the scroll bar. Look on the right-hand side of the Notepad window and you'll see small arrowhead buttons at the top and bottom and a marker in the middle. To move one line at a time, move the mouse pointer over one of the arrow buttons and click once.

4 To move several lines at a time, you can use the mouse to drag the marker up and down the bar. Move your mouse pointer over the marker, press and hold down the left mouse button and, with the button held down, slowly move the mouse. As you move the marker, you will notice the text in the Notepad window scrolls to show you where you are. Release the button.

5 You'll often want to move the whole window to another part of the Desktop. To move the Notepad window, move the mouse pointer on to the dark blue bar at the top of the window (this is the Title bar). Press and hold down the left mouse button and move the mouse – you will see that an outline of the window moves as you move the mouse. Release the button, and the Notepad window moves to the new position.

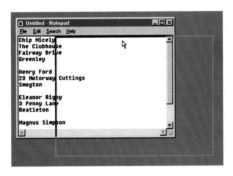

6 To see more of the text, you can make the window bigger. Move the pointer to the bottom edge of the window and it changes shape into a double-headed arrow. Press and hold down the left mouse button and drag the outline of the window to its new size. You can do the same to the sides of the window.

7 You'll have noticed that you can only change either the width or height of the window at one time by using the edges of the window. To change both, move the pointer to the bottom right corner of the window and you'll see it change to a diagonal arrow. Press and hold down the left mouse button and drag the window to its new shape.

8 To make the window as large as possible, use the Maximize button. Move the mouse button to the middle of the three small buttons in the top right corner of the window. Click once and the window will stretch to fill the whole screen.

9 Once the window is maximized, you will see that the button you just pressed looks different. If you click on the new button, the Notepad window will return to its previous size. This is known as the Restore button.

Switching between windows

Windows lets you run several programs at the same time, switching between them as you like. In this exercise, you'll see how to start another program – Calculator – that Windows will run at the same time as the Notepad program.

1 Calculator is a useful program that works just like a desktop calculator. Let's start this so that you have two programs running at the same time. Click on the Start button, move to Programs, then to Accessories, then down to the Calculator entry. Click once with the left mouse button.

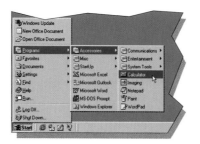

2 The Calculator tool will start and is displayed on the screen in its own window. Notice that another button appears on the Taskbar for this new program.

3 Depending on where your Notepad window is, you might find that the Calculator program has opened on top of the Notepad window. This often happens when you start up a new program, so being able to switch between windows and programs is an essential part of becoming a more proficient Windows user.

If Calculator has not appeared on top of Notepad, move the Calculator window by dragging it with the mouse, just as you did for Notepad in step 5 of the exercise on page 11.

4 At the moment, Calculator is active and has a blue Title bar. Move the mouse pointer onto any part of the Notepad window that is visible and click once. The Notepad window becomes active; its Title bar changes to blue and it appears on top of Calculator.

A quick way to switch programs is a special keyboard shortcut. Press the [Alt] key and keep it pressed. Now press the [Tab] key. You'll see a small panel appear in the middle of the screen with icons for each of the windows you have open. Each time you press the [Tab] key a box will outline the next icon. When you have selected the icon for the program you want, just release the [Alt] key.

5 An alternative way of switching between several programs is to use the Taskbar. If you look at the Taskbar, it has the Start button, a button for Notepad and a third for Calculator. To make Calculator active again, move the pointer over the Calculator button on the Taskbar and click once with the left mouse button.

6 Notice that when a window is active – in other words, the one that appears to be on top on your computer screen – its button appears pushed in. Click on the Notepad button, and Notepad moves to the top again. This is a very effective way to switch between windows and programs when you have several open.

7 Often you will want to clear your Windows Desktop of windows and programs without actually closing them. This reduces clutter and helps you to find a particular program that is buried under a stack of other windows. Windows makes this easy; you can minimize a window – reduce it to just a button on the Taskbar, with no window on the rest of the screen – by clicking on the first of the three buttons at the top right of the window. The window shrinks to the bottom of the screen.

8 Sometimes you will want to minimize all of your windows – perhaps to work with some of the Windows Desktop icons, but without closing all the programs you are currently using. In Windows 98 you can press the Taskbar's Show Desktop button to minimize all windows quickly. When you have finished working on the Desktop, it's a simple matter of pressing the button you want to work with to switch directly to that program.

Closing programs correctly

When you have finished using a program, you need to know how to close it. It is exactly the same with your computer. If you do not shut down either your program or computer in the correct way, you could damage your files or slow down your PC's performance.

1 Close down the Calculator. To close a program, move the mouse pointer to the small X button in the top right of the window and click once. All Windows programs can be closed in this way.

2 Move to the Notepad window (using the button on the Taskbar if the window is not visible) and close this program using the X button in the top-right corner.

3 If you have not saved your work, the program will warn you and ask if you want to save it. A dialog box pops up with three buttons:
• The Yes button lets you save your work.
• The No button lets you close Notepad and discard the work.
• The Cancel button lets you return to Notepad so you can check to see whether you need to save your work or not.
  We want to save the text in a file, so click on the Yes button.

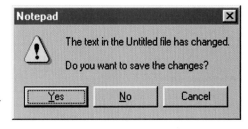

4 A new window is displayed, with the title Save As. This has several elements, but the main part of the window will list any files and folders in the My Documents folder on your hard disk drive.

5 Below this is a space where you can type in the name of the file. Let's save the names and addresses in their own file called 'My Names and Addresses' – type this into the space labeled File name.

6 Press the Save button to save the file. As soon as you press the button, Notepad stores your work to the hard disk and closes.

7 When you have finished using your computer, it is important that you shut it down correctly. When you shut down Windows, it carries out vital checks to make sure all your files are safe. If you just switch off your computer without using the correct shut-down procedure, you could damage some files.
  To shut down Windows correctly, click on the Start button and click on the first entry in the pop-up menu, labeled Shut Down.

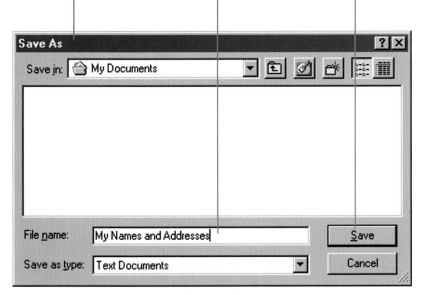

WINDOWS WARNING

Your software has lots of built-in features that help make sure you don't lose your work. Whenever you close a program, it checks to see if there have been any changes since it was last saved. Always think twice before clicking the No button. Press it and all work since the last save will be lost.

8 Once you have selected the Shut Down entry, you'll see a window with three or more options. These allow you to shut down the computer, restart the computer (sometimes needed immediately after you have added new software) and restart your computer in a special mode that we shall explain later in the course. Your PC may also have a standby mode or offer the ability to log on to other users.
  Most of the time you'll select Shut down (the default option) and click on the OK button. Windows then deletes any temporary files set up during this computing session and closes down any applications that are running. After a few seconds, Windows will tell you that it's safe to turn off your computer. If you have a newer PC, it might even turn off automatically!

Using drag and drop

Drag and drop is an essential technique that you can use in a wide range of Windows programs. Master your mouse and organize your Desktop by following these simple operations.

If you want to become an efficient Windows user, you will need to learn to control and use your mouse like an expert. Don't worry, the mouse is a friendly tool; there are just a few extra techniques to master to get the most out of Windows. Among the more useful mousing skills is a technique called 'drag and drop'.

So what is drag and drop? The phrase quite simply explains what you do: you use the mouse to select a Windows object, drag it around the screen and drop it into a new position. It's easy to learn and you'll find that you do it almost every time you use Windows. The same technique is used in many other programs.

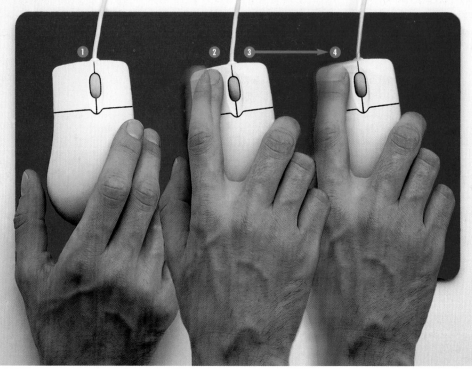

● Drop everything
You can drag and drop all sorts of objects in Windows: for example, you can use it to move icons, files, windows and even the Taskbar. In programs, there are other objects you can drag and drop, such as sections of text in word processors (Word), cells in spreadsheets (Excel) and parts of pictures in graphics programs (Paint).

● Let's do it
Before you can drag and drop an object, you first have to select it. This is simple and you've probably already done it without realizing it. Why not try it now? Go to the Windows Desktop and position the mouse pointer over the My Computer icon. To select it, all you need to do is click the left mouse button. Note that the icon and the text below it are highlighted in a new color – usually dark blue.

Now click somewhere else on the background of the Windows Desktop to de-select the My Computer icon. Notice how the icon and its text label are no longer highlighted in color.

● Change position
Let's select the My Computer icon again, but this time instead of just clicking the left mouse button, press it and hold it down. We're going to use drag and drop to move the My Computer icon to a new position on the Desktop.

First, let's drag it: keep the left mouse button pressed down and move your mouse as if you were using it to move the pointer. Notice how the pointer changes to a shaded image of the icon as you move it around the screen with the mouse – the original icon stays where it was.

Now for the drop: keep the mouse button pressed down and drag the My Computer icon to a new position on the screen. Then all you have to do is simply release the mouse button. This will leave the icon in its new place.

This is called dropping. Notice how the icon automatically disappears from its old position and reappears in the place where you dropped it.

Drag and drop is a Windows technique. Here's how to do it:
1 *Position the mouse.*
2 *Click the left mouse button.*
3 *Drag the mouse to the required position.*
4 *Drop by releasing the left mouse button.*

SHORT CUTS

Here's a fast way to close a program, a window or Windows itself: press [Alt]+[F4]. This will close the current window. If no windows are active, it will bring up the Shut Down Windows dialog box.

Windows will tell you where you cannot drop items by adding a 'restricted access' symbol to the outline of the icon you are dragging.

● **Restricted areas**

There are some areas of the Desktop where you aren't allowed to drag and drop objects. You needn't worry, however, Windows will warn you if you are doing anything that you shouldn't – you can't break anything.

Try it. Click on the My Computer icon, hold down the left button and try to drag and drop the icon onto the Recycle Bin. As you drag it over the bin, a restricted area symbol – a circle with a diagonal line across it – appears. If you try to drop the icon there, you'll see how Windows simply ignores your request and returns the icon to its original position.

SPECIAL SHORTCUTS

When you follow the exercise below, you'll see that the new icon on the Desktop looks just like the original (C:) icon, except for a small arrow in its bottom left corner. Windows also adds 'Shortcut to' to the original icon's text label. Try the icon and you'll find that it works just like the original. So what's the difference?

A shortcut is a pointer to the original, used to make things more convenient for you. You can add as many as you like and put them almost anywhere you like. If you delete them, the original remains safe. Many Windows users like to add Desktop shortcuts for their favorite programs to reduce the need to hunt around for them.

Dragging and dropping Windows shortcuts

Mastering this basic Windows technique will make you much more productive. In this example, we'll add a shortcut to your Windows Desktop that will give you fast access to your hard disk.

1 As you use your computer, you'll notice that the My Computer icon is one of the most common Desktop items you use. It contains icons for many useful programs and windows, including your disk drives (A:, C: and D:).

2 Double-click on the My Computer icon and its window opens to show your PC's disk drives and some other folders (don't worry about these for now). We want to add an icon for our hard disk (C:) to our Desktop.

3 Click on the (C:) icon and keep the button pressed down. The icon will be highlighted. While the button is still down, drag the pointer to the Desktop, just to the right of the My Computer icon. Notice how the pointer shows you have picked up the icon. Drop the icon by letting go of the button when it is in the position you want.

4 As soon as you let go of the mouse button, a Yes/No dialog box pops up and asks you if you want to create a shortcut. We want to make a shortcut for our hard disk (see Special Shortcuts, above), so click on the Yes button.

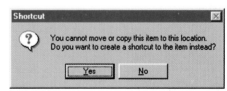

5 You can now see a new icon on your Desktop, labeled 'Shortcut to (C)'. It works exactly like the (C:) icon in the My Computer window, but now it's available right from the moment you start Windows.

6 You can also add icons for your floppy disk and CD-ROM drives. Repeat steps 3 to 5 for each of the drives you want to add. Remember, if you want to move them once they are on the Desktop, you can just drag and drop them as necessary.

Introducing the Clipboard

The Clipboard is one of Windows' best features; it makes copying words, numbers and pictures between documents easy. Here's how to use the Clipboard's built-in intelligence to get more out of Windows.

As you work with Windows programs, you'll find you often need to move information from one part of a document to another. Perhaps you need to duplicate the same words several times, or maybe you need to copy most of the text from one letter to a different letter.

The good news is that Windows has a special feature that makes all this easy. Forget laborious retyping – with a few simple commands the Clipboard can do it all. It can even copy pictures or tables of numbers.

● What is the Clipboard?
The Clipboard is a special area of your PC's memory that can hold a temporary copy of any information you like. You first choose the information you want to copy, and then get Windows to copy it to the Clipboard. Then you choose where you want it to

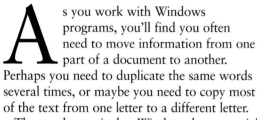

go and get Windows to paste it from the Clipboard to the new position.

● Select to copy
The key to letting Windows know what you want to copy is to make sure you select it. You can try this right now in Windows' simple word processing program, WordPad.

In WordPad, type a few sentences. Choose some words that you wish to copy to another part of the page. Put the mouse pointer just in front of the word, press and hold the left mouse button, drag the mouse to the end of the word and release the button.

Take note that as you drag the mouse, the text you have selected changes from black letters on white to white letters on black (see right). Then you need to copy it to the Clipboard. Click on the Edit menu, then click on the Copy command from the drop-down list that appears. It looks like nothing has happened, but Clipboard now has a copy of your text.

● Paste the word
Choose where you want the word to go. Put the mouse pointer at the required position and click once. The word you originally selected reverts to black text on a white background, and the insertion point moves to the new position. Click on the Edit menu, then click on the Paste command in the drop-down list. The copied text appears at the indicated location in the document.

Cutting, copying and pasting with the Windows Clipboard takes the drudgery out of repetitive documents. Make retyping a thing of the past by getting to grips with your program's Edit menu.

PC TIPS

There's another bonus to using the Clipboard: you can eliminate repetitive typing. That's because you can paste information as many times as you like once it's in the Clipboard. Just keep clicking on Paste until you're done!
Note: there may be times when you want to remove the text from its original position. To do this, click on Cut from the Edit menu instead of Copy.
You will see the selected words disappear from the document, and you can paste them straight into the new position as usual.

Copying from program to program

On the opposite page you saw how to cut, copy and paste text in WordPad. Now let's see how easy it is to use the Clipboard in an especially useful way: to copy information from one program to another.

1 Start WordPad and Calculator (they're both in the Accessories folder in the Programs folder of the Start menu).

Move and resize the WordPad window until the two programs are side by side as shown here. If you're not sure how to move and resize a window, refer to the exercise on page 11.

2 Copy this sample letter in WordPad. To complete the letter, you'll need to work out how much the payments will come to.

All you have to do is move the mouse pointer to the Calculator window, click somewhere on it to make it active, and then you can work out the calculation.

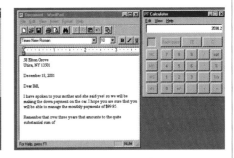

3 You can use either the numerical keypad or just click the mouse on Calculator's buttons. (Make sure the [NumLock] key is pressed and its light on the keyboard is lit before you try to use these keys.) Enter the following calculation: '99.95*36='
The Calculator display will give you the exact answer as soon as you click the [=] button.

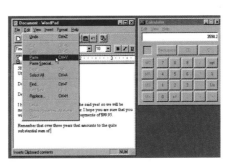

4 Now you know the answer, you could just retype the answer into WordPad, but that presents the risk of a typing mistake. Instead, we'll use the Windows Clipboard to store the answer.

Click on Calculator's Edit menu and click on Copy from the drop-down list. Note: in this particular case, you don't even need to select the answer before copying.

5 Switch to the WordPad window by clicking inside it, and position the insertion point at the appropriate position by clicking the I-beam pointer just to the right of the last line in the WordPad window.

Click on the word Edit in the menu bar and click Paste from the drop-down command list. An exact copy of the answer to the calculation is copied into your WordPad document.

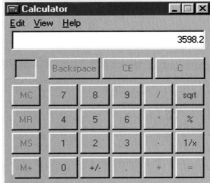

6 Many programs accept other types of information from the Clipboard. Switch to the Calculator and press [Alt]+[PrintScreen]. This copies a picture of the Calculator to the Clipboard. Go back to WordPad and position the insertion point at the end of the document.

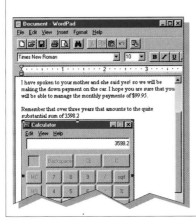

7 Now use the same Edit and Paste commands from WordPad's menus as you did in step 5. The Windows Clipboard knows that WordPad can handle pictures just as well as text, and it pastes a picture of the Calculator window into the document at the position of the cursor. This is a very useful trick we'll look at in detail later in the course. (Note: you can change the size of the picture by clicking and dragging any of the eight square 'handles' on the edges of the picture.)

Save the letter into the My Documents folder, following the steps on page 13.

PC TIPS

The right mouse button

Your mouse can help when cutting and pasting. Instead of moving the pointer to the Edit menu, you can select the text you wish to move, then click the right mouse button.

This brings up a menu of options, including Cut, Copy and Paste, which you can use in exactly the same way as the Edit menu options.

Understanding files and folders

Your computer's hard disk can store thousands of letters, pictures and programs. All these files can easily clutter up a system, so to keep it all organized and manageable, Windows uses folders. Here's an explanation of how files and folders work.

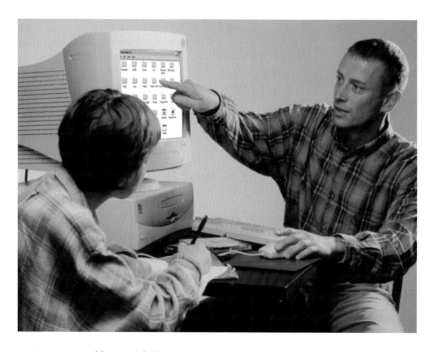

A computer is like an electronic office, and your data and work are stored in Windows much the same as papers are stored in an office. Just as an office has hundreds of documents, and therefore requires a filing system, so your computer also needs a filing system to keep track of all your work.

The key to understanding how your computer manages files – which can be programs, letters, pictures and so on – is to compare it to the way documents in an office are stored. You'll see there are plenty of similarities; the only real differences are because your computer is much more flexible and powerful than office filing systems.

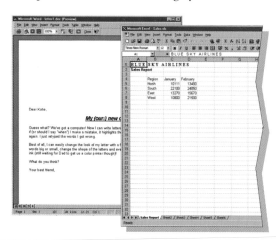

Every time you save a letter, spreadsheet or other document, you create a file on your hard disk. Windows lets you store these files in electronic folders so that you can avoid disorganized clutter.

● Documents, files and folders

An ordinary office has many types of document, from single page letters and photographs to multipage reports. It's usual – and often essential – to keep related documents together in a folder. These folders might also be stored within other objects, such as a filing cabinet, for example.

Your computer works in just the same way. The basic unit for storing computer information is a file. This is exactly equivalent to the office document: photographs, letters, reports and so on (programs on your PC are also stored as files).

● Don't worry about size

Windows also lets you keep related files together in folders – just like at the office. The big difference is that you don't have to worry about the physical size of your documents and folders. Putting a three-inch thick report into a one-inch thick folder is impossible in

If you share your PC with your family, it's important to make sure everyone understands the basic principles concerning files and folders on your hard disk.

real life, but Windows will let you put huge files into a folder. This electronic folder will happily swallow whatever you put in it. You can also put folders into folders – almost impossible with real-life manila folders.

Just as every office worker makes sure to label files and folders with a name or number for easy storage and retrieval, so Windows makes sure files have names: 'letter to grandma' or 'cat photo 1', for instance. Depending on how your PC is set up, you may also see three letters tacked onto the end of a file's name. This is called an extension and lets Windows know what type of file it is. A .doc extension would be for a Word document, for instance.

● Disks and filing cabinets

All your files and folders are stored on disks in your computer (floppy disk, hard disk and CD-ROM). The only real limitation on the number of documents such disks can contain is the amount of space the files take up. Rather like a storeroom in an office, a disk starts off empty, but can become packed over time with programs, letters and other documents (see pages 96–97).

In the step-by-step guide below, you can see how the folders and files stored on your computer appear through Windows. On page 21, we show you how to create and use your own folders.

Exploring files and folders on your hard disk

Find out how files and folders work by browsing through your hard disk.

1 Start your exploration of your files and folders by double-clicking on the My Computer icon on the Windows Desktop.

2 You'll see a new window that shows icons for the disk drives in your PC together with a collection of other icons. Double-click on the [C:] icon, which represents your hard disk, to see what's stored there.

3 The window that pops open shows the files and folders stored on your hard disk (the exact number and type depends on how many you have created and the software you have). Folders look like miniature versions of the manila folders you'll find in every office (above right). Files look like miniature pictures of various types of documents (left).

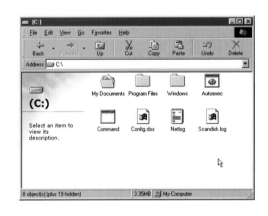

4 Double-click on the Program Files folder to see what's inside. You'll see something like this: a collection of file folders (they are called subfolders) for the programs installed on your computer. Just browse through these subfolders for a moment – don't click on any of the files inside the folders. Use the toolbar's Back and Up buttons to retrace your steps. Close the window by clicking on the X button at its top-right corner.

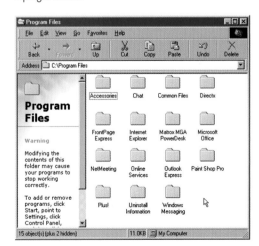

There are two ways to store your work: the messy way, where you can never find anything, and the organized way. Organize your computer now and you'll save time in the long run.

Managing files and folders

You can save your files anywhere on your hard disk, but if you want to be able to find them again easily, it is best to use the tools provided in Windows to create folders and organize your files logically. This is a more efficient way to work that will save you a lot of time and avoid unnecessary problems.

If you share your computer with other members of the family, you can give everyone their own personal folders. That way, you can minimize the amount of confusion caused if you want to save files with similar names. You can also store important files out of harm's way, leaving children with their own folders to work and play in.

● Organized chaos

Think about how you organize your paperwork and documents at home or work. You don't just pile them all in one place. Ideally, you group them by subject headings and store them in separate folders with easy-to-remember names.

This is also the best way to store your files in Windows. As you'll see in the step-by-step guide opposite, it's simple to create a folder for any subject you're working on and save the relevant files in it. Unlike real folders, computer folders are free!

After a while, you may find your folders become cluttered with lots of files, but don't worry because you can always create sub-folders of your folder and move files from one folder to another any time you like.

● Folders make life easier

Once you've created your folders, you can move them around your hard disk as easily as any type of file. A big advantage of this is that when you want to move a folder – perhaps to make a copy on a floppy disk – all the files and folders inside it will be copied, too.

Just as there seems to be no end to the number of Russian dolls that can fit inside each other, you can continue to put files and folders into other folders on your hard disk as many times as you like.

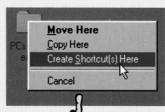

Creating and using a new folder

Here's how to create your own *PCs made easy* folder on your hard disk.
Once it is created, you can start organizing your documents by copying
and moving files you have already saved on your hard disk.

1 To start, double-click with the left mouse
button on the My Computer icon on your
Windows Desktop. When the My Computer
window opens, double-click on the [C:] drive,
which represents your hard disk.

2 Your hard disk contains lots of files and
folders. To create a new folder, click on
the File menu, select the New option and then
click on the Folder command from the second
list that appears.

3 The new folder is simply called New
Folder, but you can type over this label
with the name you want the folder to have.
In this case, type in *PCs made easy* and press
the [Enter] key.

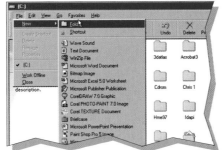

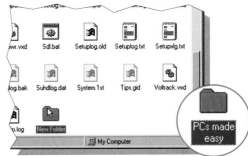

4 Double-click on the
new *PCs made
easy* folder to open its
window and repeat steps
2 and 3 to create a new
folder inside it. This time
name it Word.

5 Now you can move one of the files you have created
into your new folder. Open the My Documents folder
from the My Computer window. Move the My Documents
and *PCs made easy* windows until they are side by side.
Click on one of the files: we've chosen a Word document
called 'acceptance letter.doc'. You could use one of the files
you have already saved (see pages 13 and 17).

6 Drag the file icon from the My Documents window
to the Word folder in the *PCs made easy* window.
As the mouse pointer moves over the yellow Word folder,
note that the folder becomes highlighted to show that is
where the file will go when you drop it. Drop the icon on
the folder.

7 Notice that the original icon for the file you have moved disappears
from the My Documents window. That is because Windows made an
intelligent guess that because you dragged the file icon to a place on the
same disk, you wanted to move it and not copy it. Most of the time this is
correct, but sometimes you will want to keep the original in the same place.

8 Copying a file, rather than moving it, is a simple matter of
pressing the [Ctrl] key during the drag-and-drop operation. Try it
now with one of the other documents from your My Documents
window. You'll see that the icon you are dragging with the mouse
pointer has a small + sign next to it. Windows uses this to indicate that
the file being dragged is 'in addition' to the original. Drop the icon on
the Word folder and the original stays in place.

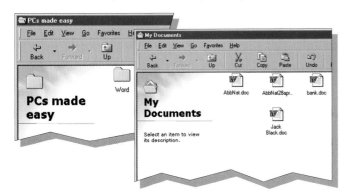

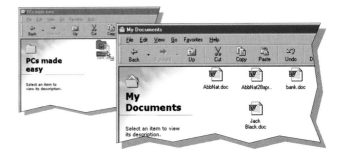

Directories and paths

Learning to find your way around the numerous folders on your hard drive is a useful skill. Once you understand the logical structure, you will never have trouble finding a file again.

On pages 18–21, you looked at the concept of folders, which form the basic building blocks for storing your files and documents on your PC. However, you might have wondered how these files and folders are stored on your hard disk and how they are organized. To know this you need to understand the concepts behind directories and paths.

● Branching out

The structure of the many different files and folders on your hard disk is often called a directory tree. The analogy of a tree, with its roots and branches, is quite a useful one. The root of the tree is equivalent to the root directory, the most basic level of your hard disk.

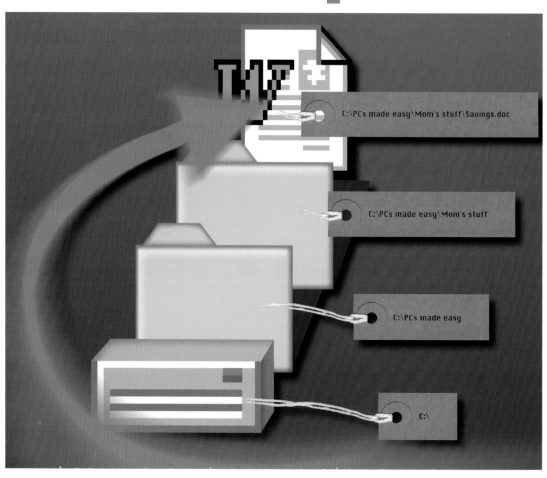

C:\PCs made easy\Mom's stuff\Savings.doc

C:\PCs made easy\Mom's stuff

C:\PCs made easy

C:\

Understanding how files and folders end up where they do on your hard disk will help you manage your computer more effectively and efficiently.

Just as a tree has branches, so your hard disk has folders, or directories. And as the branches of a tree can split into many more branches, so the directories on your hard disk can branch off into further directories. These branches are not predetermined when you buy your computer – you create them as you install software or make folders in which to store your own files and documents. There are very few limitations on how you develop your directories – you can create as many levels as you need.

● Descriptive path

Most of the time you navigate your way around the hard disk by double-clicking on folder icons. Sometimes, however, it's better to describe the location of a file or folder as a simple line of text which indicates the route, or 'path', to the file/folder as it branches off from the root. It will help you to understand this more fully if you go through the step-by-step exercise opposite.

Following the file path

When you understand just a little about paths and directories it will be easier both to store and find files on your computer.

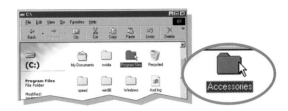

1 Double-click on the My Computer icon on the Desktop. You'll see the usual collection of hardware devices and special folders, in addition to the disk drives on your computer. Double-click on the hard disk icon (usually labeled [C:]) to see the contents of the root directory.

2 When the new window appears, look at the Title bar. If you see C: instead of C:\, use the PC Tips (below left) so that you can see the full path in the Title bar.

3 Find the Program Files folder and double-click on that. The new Title bar will show that you are in the C:\Program Files directory. Find the Accessories folder (inset right) and double-click on it.

PC TIPS

If you want to know the path of folders as you navigate through them, there is an option in Windows to display the full path in the Title bar of any folder. To do so, go to the View menu and choose Folder Options. Click on the View tab and click with the mouse to put a check mark next to the option called Display the full path in title bar.

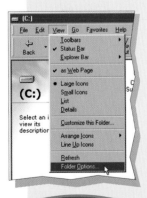

4 When the window appears, the path in the Title bar changes to show C:\Program Files\Accessories. Windows has used the backslash (\) character between Program Files and Accessories to indicate different levels of directory.

5 The Wordpad program (Wordpad.exe) is stored in this folder. Drag it onto the Desktop. This will make a shortcut (see page 15), which you can use to start the program directly from the Desktop.

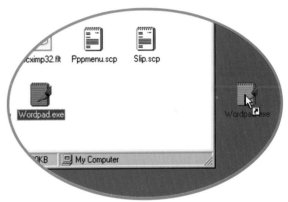

6 Right-click on the new shortcut for the Wordpad program and select the Properties option from the drop-down menu that appears.

7 Click on the Shortcut tab of the dialog box (right) and you'll see that the Target text box shows you the exact path of the Wordpad program file. The full path includes the disk drive (C:), the route through the folders you double-clicked on (\Program Files\Accessories) and the name of the file, which in our example is Wordpad.exe.

Windows programs use paths to keep track of the files and folders they are working with. In addition, paths can be used to refer directly to your documents.

TARGETS AND PATHS

When you create a shortcut, you are telling Windows to go to a specific place on your hard drive. This place is called a Target and Windows creates a path to it. Windows uses the Target when you double-click on a shortcut. The Target retraces the path through the folders to find and start the program.

Windows Explorer

Most of the time, it's easy to open the My Computer icon and then click on the objects and folders within it to look through the files and folders stored on your computer. However, if you find that the Desktop gets cluttered when you've got several windows open, take a look at the Windows Explorer which brings them all together in a single window.

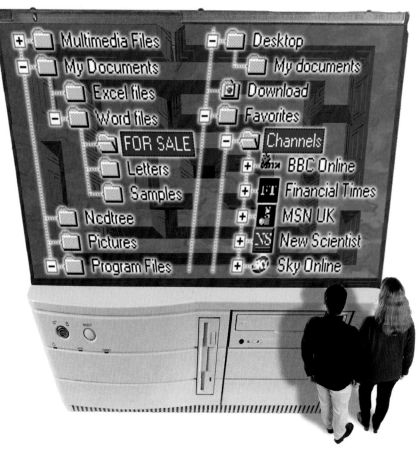

By now, you should be experienced at opening and using the My Computer icon in Windows to explore your PC and look at the files, folders and other objects stored on your hard disk, floppy disk and CD-ROM drives. The My Computer icon is really easy to use – all you have to do is double-click on it to open the My Computer window. This window contains large icons that represent your computer's hard disk, the floppy disk drive, the CD-ROM drive and a handful of other icons that control how your computer works.

● Inside your computer

If you're interested in seeing what files and folders are stored on your hard disk, all you have to do is double-click on the large icon that represents the hard disk; it's usually called (C:). Then Windows will open a new window that shows icons for the top level of files and folders stored on the hard disk. If you want to examine the contents of a particular folder, all you have to do is double-click on its icon and Windows will open another window that contains icons for each file and subfolder within that folder.

This simple-to-understand technique has only one real drawback: your Desktop can soon get cluttered if you open lots of windows. You often have to move the various windows around on screen to see the contents

of the folders you're interested in. However, Windows includes another tool that you can use to view your files and folders. This other tool avoids unwanted clutter: it's called Windows Explorer.

To see how Explorer works, click on the Start button in the Windows Taskbar and choose Programs. Now choose the Windows Explorer option from the menu that appears (the icon beside it looks like a magnifying glass over a folder).

● Explorer panes

The Windows Explorer window is split into two parts, usually referred to as panes. The left pane contains icons for all the main parts of your computer, such as the Desktop, hard disk drive, floppy disk drive and CD-ROM drive. Click once on the hard disk icon (C:) in the left pane, and the right pane fills up with icons for the top-level files and folders on your hard disk.

Double-click on one of these folders and the contents of the right pane will change to show the contents of that folder. You'll notice how, at the same time, the left pane changes to show a tree view of the hard disk: you can see all the folders it contains.

As we'll see in the exercises on the next three pages, the Windows Explorer is a powerful way of exploring your computer in a single window.

WHAT IT MEANS

TREE VIEW
This describes the hierarchical view of the disks, files and folders stored on the PC. Windows Explorer represents your PC as a tree of objects stored inside other objects. Each part of your PC (for example, the hard disk) is a branch. Every folder within one of these branches is treated as a subbranch, and so on down to individual files.

A tree view of your computer

To keep tabs on a huge collection of loose documents, folders and objects, Windows files all your contents hierarchically.

THE TREE VIEW used in Windows Explorer views the Desktop as the top level of the hierarchy of your PC, with everything else as an element on the Desktop. For example, the My Computer icon, which represents the hardware components of your PC, is treated as an item on the Desktop.

The next level below this in the hierarchy contains components that can store data such as files, folders and other objects. This also includes items such as your hard disk, floppy disk and CD-ROM drives. Also included are the tools, such as the Control Panel, that allow you to set up other items of hardware inside or connected to your PC.

Below this, each component that can store data has its own, separate, hierarchical structure of folders that can contain files and subfolders which, in turn, can contain more files and subfolders.

Even though the words 'hierarchical structure' and 'top level view' may sound like computer jargon, they make sense when you see a graphical representation of the way your files and folders are organized by Windows.

You can see in this diagram how the hierarchy works. My Computer is the top level (in reality, the Windows Desktop is the top level), and below this is the treelike structure of files and folders. At the next level down are the three icons that represent the floppy disk, hard disk and CD-ROM drives. Assuming we don't have a floppy or CD-ROM disk inserted, we continue down the hierarchy through the hard disk drive and see a 'branch' of five folders. We follow the hierarchy through the PCs made easy folder, where we see folders for Excel and Word files and a Paint file (Map1.bmp).

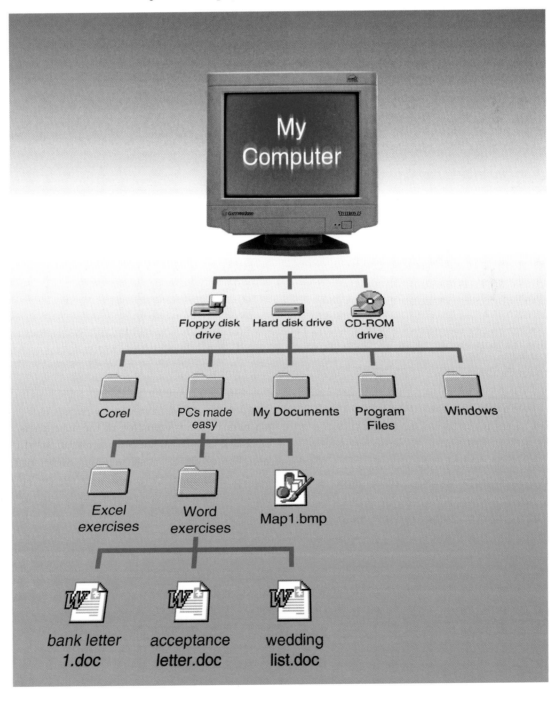

Viewing files and folders with Explorer

Use a handy shortcut in Windows Explorer to see how the items on your computer are related to each other.

1 From the Windows Desktop, use the right mouse button to click on the My Computer icon and select Explore from the menu of options that appears.

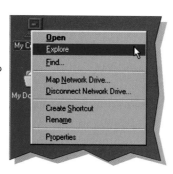

2 Notice how the Windows Explorer window is split into two panes. The left pane shows the top-level parts of your computer (such as the hard disk). When you first open Explorer, this structure is duplicated in the right pane. Now click once on the hard disk icon in the left pane.

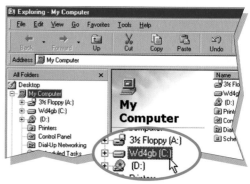

3 The right pane changes to show lots of icons – one for each object stored at the next level down in the hierarchy of your hard disk. Double-click on the Program Files folder in the right pane.

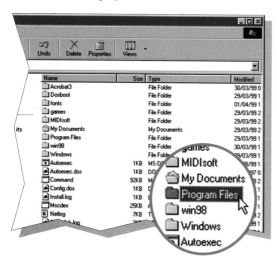

4 The right pane will change to show icons for all the files and folders held in the Program Files folder. You can also see a short warning in the center of the window. This alerts you to problems that might occur if you change or delete files or folders in the Program Files folder.

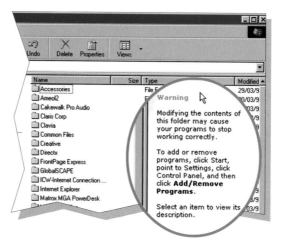

5 Exploring without making changes is fine, however. Double-click on the Accessories folder. The right pane shows the contents of the Accessories folder and the left pane shows the next level down in the tree structure. Notice how the Accessories folder icon in the left pane is open as a reminder.

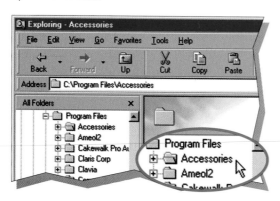

6 So that's how you move down the tree structure in Windows Explorer, but how do you get back up? That's just as easy: all you have to do is click on the Up button folder shape in the toolbar at the top of the Explorer window.

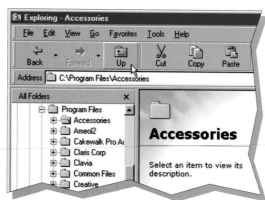

PC TIPS

Opening folders quickly

If you work through the exercise on this page, you might notice that little plus and minus signs keep appearing and disappearing beside the folder icons in the left pane of Explorer. When a plus sign appears beside a folder, it means that the folder contains subfolders. The quick way to see these subfolders is to click on the plus sign. Explorer will then show them in the left pane as the next level of the tree view.

When you do this, the plus sign changes to a minus sign. Click on the minus sign to close the folder. This technique also works for icons that represent other types of objects in Explorer, such as the Desktop itself, the hard disk and the CD-ROM drive.

Choosing different views

If you're happy with the large icons that you usually see in the My Computer window, you can get Windows Explorer to show files and objects information in the same way.

THERE ARE obvious differences between the way things look and behave when you use Windows Explorer, compared to the look of files and folders in the method we've seen before when using the My Computer icon. For a start, everything happens in one window with a tree view when you use Explorer, as opposed to a separate window for each folder when you use the My Computer icon. These are just two ways of looking at the same information.

Here is how you can alter the right pane of the Windows Explorer view; the left pane always shows the tree view with small icons.

1 Windows Explorer has a toolbar that gives you ways to alter its appearance with a single click. If the toolbar isn't visible when you start Explorer, go to the View menu, click Toolbars and select Standard Buttons from the submenu.

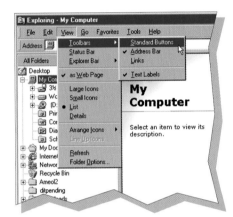

2 The Views button on the far right of the toolbar gives you control over Explorer's appearance. The selected view option here is List, which shows a simple list of files, folders and other objects in the right pane with small icons beside them.

3 If you want to see more information about each object in the right pane, you'll need to select the Details option. To do this, click the downward pointing arrow next to the Views button and select Details.

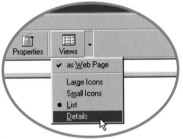

4 The right panel changes to show extra columns of information. You can explore your files and folders in this view, or try another.

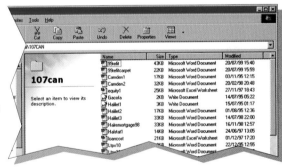

5 Windows Explorer can show items in the right pane as large icons, too. Select Large Icons using the Views button. The downside of the Large Icons view is that they take up a lot of space. Try the Small Icons option if this is a problem.

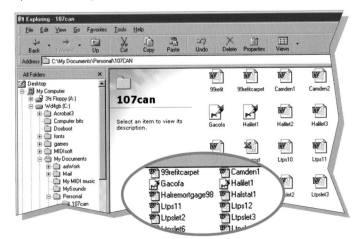

PC TIPS

You can use the Properties button on the toolbar to see information about any of the items in either of the panes of the Explorer window. Select an item and press Properties. A window then gives you information about the item, including its size and what it contains (inset right). You can also access the Properties box by clicking on an item with the right mouse button and choosing it from the menu.

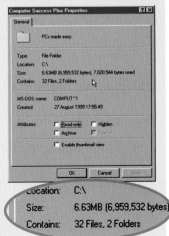

Software

Microsoft®Paint

Success with words

Word processing – creating text documents on a computer – is the most frequently performed task on a PC. In PCs made easy, we take you step-by-step through one of the top programs in the field, Microsoft Word.

Word processing is the term used to describe all the activities associated with creating text documents on a computer. This covers letters, résumés, reports and memos, flyers and school or office projects; in fact, almost any form of written document. The beauty of word processing is that once you have typed your document, you can save it, alter the look of it using the many tools built into each program, and print out as many copies as you need.

● Improving features

Microsoft Word is one of the most popular word processing programs on the market. The program has been around for a long time, but it is constantly being improved and updated with new features. Don't worry if you have a slightly different version of Microsoft Word to the one shown on the opposite page, or even if you have another program, such as WordPerfect. Its menus or toolbars might look

different, but the same basic principles of word processing still apply.

● First words

With a word processor, you can correct any mistakes you make before you print your document, move around a document quickly using your mouse, delete and reposition individual words or blocks of text, and even check your spelling. To alter the appearance of your finished document, you can change the margins and format of your pages. You can make some of the text bold, italic or even put it all into a different typeface. The list of features goes on and the possibilities are huge. The more you use a word processor, the more you will realize its potential.

The first thing to learn in Microsoft Word is where all these tools and functions are located. On the following pages, we shall guide you through the process of opening a blank page in Word, and taking the initial steps toward creating your first letter.

THE [ENTER] KEY

This is the large key just to the right of the main set of letter keys, next to the square bracket [ ] keys. It's also known as the [Return] key. This key is also repeated at the bottom right of the numeric keypad.

Making a start on a blank page

It's now time to start Microsoft Word from Windows and introduce you to all the main features of the word processing program. Have your mouse ready.

TO BEGIN working on a Word document you first have to start the program. This is simple. Switch on your computer and monitor, and wait until Windows appears.

Using your mouse, put the pointer on the Start menu in the left corner of the screen and click with the left button.

A pop-up menu will appear. From the list, choose Programs. When the second menu appears, click on Microsoft Word. The Word start-up screen will appear, followed automatically by a blank page. This is your first document, called Document1. The words and buttons you can see are the tools with which you control the program.

Toolbars

Toolbars are very useful. They feature icon buttons that allow you to give the program commands without having to go through the pull-down menus. Microsoft Word has many different toolbars, which you can hide or display, depending on the task you want to perform.

Menu bar

The nine subjects on this bar each give access to a pull-down menu. Simply click on a word to reveal the list of commands under each subject.

Title bar

The line of text at the top of the screen that shows the program you are using (Microsoft Word) and the name of your file ('Document1').

Standard toolbar

This contains the most commonly used command buttons, such as the ones that open and close documents, print, check the spelling and cut and paste the text.

Formatting toolbar

Situated below the Standard toolbar, the Formatting toolbar alters font (typeface) type and size, makes highlighted text bold, italic or underlines it, creates indents and generally helps you shape the look of your document.

Ruler

This appears below the Formatting toolbar and can be used to alter tabs and margins on a typed document.

Insertion point

A flashing vertical line that appears on the page to show where any text you type will be inserted.

Status bar

The bar at the bottom of the screen that shows further information about the document on which you are working, such as which page you are on.

Scroll bars

Gray-shaded horizontal and vertical bars at the bottom and right-hand side of a document that allow you to scroll across or down the page. There are three methods of scrolling: you can click on the vertical black arrows to move the page up or down, and click on the horizontal arrows to move the page left or right; or you can click on the gray scroll boxes within the bars, hold the left mouse button down, and drag the boxes along the bars; the third way is to click within the bars themselves and move the page in stages.

Laying out a letter

Creating documents in Microsoft Word couldn't be easier – follow these simple steps to produce your first word-processed letter.

THERE ARE times when a neatly typed letter is much more appropriate than a handwritten one, particularly in business or formal correspondence. The same applies to your résumé and job applications, reports, projects and many other documents.

The great thing about word processing programs is that you can start using them right away. All you have to do to enter text in Word is start typing. Later in the course, we will delve deeper into editing techniques such as copying and moving text, and changing the look of the words to make them stand out, but for the moment we'll keep it simple.

● Start typing

As discussed earlier, the flashing vertical line – called the text cursor or insertion point – indicates where the next character you type will appear. As you type, the insertion point moves horizontally toward the right of the screen. Unlike a typewriter, you do not have to press [Enter] every time you come to the end of a line, because the word processor automatically moves to the next line. If you

wish to separate paragraphs of text or begin a sentence on a new line, simply press the [Enter] key and the insertion point will move down a line.

● Your first letter – step 1

Try this exercise to create your first document. Start by copying the text from step 1 (below). Type it exactly as we have, pressing the [Enter] key when you want to move on to the next line. Don't worry if you make a mistake, press the [Backspace] key to remove the mistake and retype the word.

● Moving text with tabs – step 2

Now that you have completed the exercise of typing in the text, we shall show you the most simple method of converting it into letter format, as shown in step 2 (on the opposite page). When setting out a letter, it is conventional to put your own address and the date of writing on the right-hand side of the page. Rather than adding lots of spaces to move your text along the line, it is better to use the [Tab] key.

Tabs are useful if you want to create paragraph indents, align your text in columns or put measured spaces between words.

Word-processed documents are preferable to handwritten letters when entering into formal correspondence, such as applying for a new job.

[TAB] KEY

The [Tab] key is just to the left of the [Q] key. Some keyboards use an arrow and line symbol, others are printed with 'Tab.'

1 Copy the letter exactly as we have typed it. When you need to move to the next line, press the [Enter] key.

SHORTCUTS

To move the insertion point around your document, you can use a set of special keys, called cursor keys. They allow you to move the insertion point to any position on any line. The arrow on each key shows the direction that the insertion point will move when you press it.

Moves the insertion point up one line

Moves the insertion point forward one space

Moves the insertion point back one space

Moves the insertion point down one line

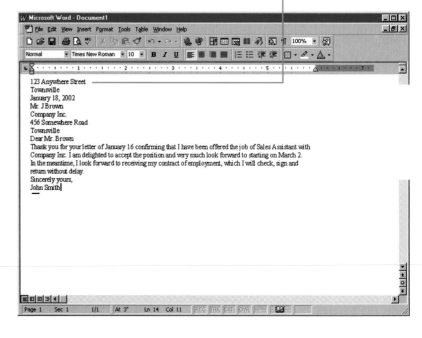

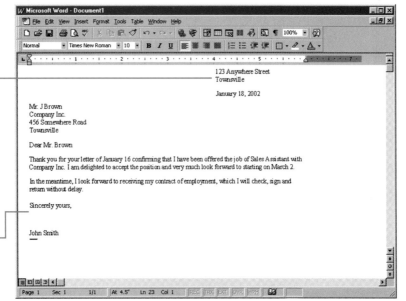

2 To format the letter, click in front of the text you want to move. In this case, it is the sender's address. Press the [Tab] key until the address and date align on the right-hand side of the page.

3 To make a blank line, all you need to do is press the [Enter] key at the beginning of an existing line.

4 After you've finished your letter, you should save it. Click on the File menu, and then click on the Save option from the drop-down menu entries.

To insert tabs, click the insertion point in front of the word or sentence you want to move, then press the [Tab] key. Word presets its tabs so that the text is moved along ½ inch (13 mm) at a time. Later in the course, we'll show you how to set tabs wherever you want them.

5 You'll see a Save As dialog box. Type a name for your letter and click on the Save button.

Keep pressing the [Tab] key until the longest line of text has moved as far to the right as it can without any of it dropping onto the next line. If you press [Tab] too many times and the text moves on to another line, simply click in front of the text and press the [Backspace] key to delete as many tabs as necessary until the whole line fits.

● Inserting blank lines – step 3

Once you have tabbed the sender's address across to the right-hand side of the page, click the insertion point just in front of the date. We want to insert a blank line between the address and the date. To do this, press the [Enter] key. This moves the text down a line. Then use the [Tab] key to move the date along until it lines up below the address.

The recipient's name and address conventionally stay on the left-hand side of the page, so insert a line space to separate it from the date. To do this, click the insertion point in front of the recipient's name (Mr. J. Brown) and press the [Enter] key again.

Follow the same procedure to insert line spaces between paragraphs until your document looks just like the one above.

Use several blank lines to give enough space to sign the letter. When you have finished, you are ready to print.

When you print out the letter, you will see that Word has added a margin to all sides of the page, so the text doesn't start quite as close to the edge of the paper as it looks on the screen. Later in the course, we'll show you how to change the margins to suit different documents.

● Saving – steps 4 & 5

After you've finished typing your letter, you should save it. Click on the File menu, and then click on the Save option. The screen that pops up – a dialog box – lets you give your letter a name. Type the name and then click the Save button. To close the Word window, click on the File menu and click Exit.

Many of the commands in Windows programs can be completed without using the pull-down menus. Most programs have quick commands that can be activated via the keyboard. Try the following shortcuts using only your control key [Ctrl] plus the letter indicated:

Create new document
[Ctrl]+N
Open document
[Ctrl]+O
Close document
[Ctrl]+W
Save document
[Ctrl]+S
Print document
[Ctrl]+P

Liven up your letters

Make your letters stand out from the crowd by adding extra flourish to your words. Here's how to use Word's Formatting toolbar to jazz up your documents with the press of a few buttons.

For many of us, letter writing is the main reason – and possibly the only time – we put words on a page. It is also the type of writing that can call for very different approaches to style.

Some types of letter – such as the job acceptance letter in the exercise on pages 32–33 – need a formal approach. You can format others in a much more informal and fun way – such as personal letters to friends and members of your family.

● Friendly formatting

One of the great things about Microsoft Word is that whatever style of letter you want to create, you use exactly the same features to achieve them, the formatting tools. There are two main groups: first, text formatting tools that change the appearance of text, and second, page formatting tools that alter the overall look of the pages.

In this exercise, we shall concentrate on how you can make your letters look attractive with the text formatting tools. With a few clicks on Word's toolbar, you can be sure that your letters will stand out from the crowd.

The Formatting toolbar

Word's toolbars give you access to many powerful commands with a single click of the mouse. Here's a guide to the most useful buttons. Use them to change the look of the text in your letters and documents.

| Normal ▼ | Times New Roman ▼ | 10 ▼ | **B** *I* <u>U</u> | ≡ ≡ ≡ ≡ | ≣ ≣ 镇 镇 | ▦ ▾ ✎ ▾ A ▾ |

Typeface
Use this drop-down list to select a typeface for your text. Click on the down arrow on the right-hand side and a list will drop down to show your choices. Scroll down this list to see more typefaces.

Text size
Use this drop-down list to select the text size. Click on the downward pointing arrow and choose the size you want. You can also change the number by clicking on it and typing a new number.

Text weight
You use these buttons to select the emphasis of the text. The B makes text bold, the I makes it italic and the U underlines it.

To turn off any of these emphasis effects, just click on the button again.

Alignment
These buttons align text. Look closely and you'll see they show the effect they have, aligning text left, centre, right or justified (on both sides). These buttons affect whole paragraphs, not just the selected text.

Others
We'll tackle the other buttons later. With them you can create special lists, change text and background colors (very useful if you have a color printer) and add borders and frames.

Adding a touch of style

Word has tools and commands to turn your plain letters into stylish and personalized letters that get you noticed. Here's a step-by-step guide to text formatting.

1 The first thing to do is open a new document and type the text of your letter. For this exercise, use the text shown here and in step 8, or use a letter you've already created.

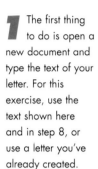

2 Let's move the address and date to the right-hand side of the page. First, select the address and date by dragging the mouse pointer from the first letter of the first line to the last letter of the date. Now click on the Align Right button on the Formatting toolbar. If you're unsure which is which, pause with the mouse pointer over each button and Word will tell you with a small yellow label.

3 Let's use the same set of buttons to center the title of the letter. Click once anywhere in the title line and then click on the Center button on the toolbar. Notice that you don't have to select the whole line.

4 We want to change the font used in the letter to a more fun one. To select all the text, click once on Edit in the menu bar and then click on Select All in the list of commands.

5 All the text changes to white on black, and now you can change the formatting of the whole document at once. To change the font, click once on the typeface list box and scroll down until you see Comic Sans MS (you might have different fonts on your computer depending on your software).

Click on the font you want and you'll see the whole letter change. Experiment with different fonts and see how they change the look of the letter.

6 To change the emphasis of the letter's title, select it (by dragging the mouse from the first letter of the title to the last) and click on the Bold, Italic and Underline tools. We have also made the address bold.

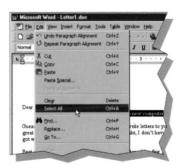

7 To make the title stand out even more, change the size of the text. With the title selected, click once on the font size list. When the list appears, select a size of about 18 (the letters will be about one quarter of an inch [6mm] tall).

8 Here's our final letter. Remember that we chose fonts and styles to add a fun appearance to our letter. You can also use exactly the same commands to choose different fonts and sizes to make letters more business-like. Experiment with some of your letters.

WHAT IT MEANS

FONT

This is printing jargon for typeface, the overall design of letters and numbers. Look at this page of PCs made easy and you can see several typefaces: most of the text is in a font called Futura Book, the headlines are Futura Condensed Bold, and this text is Sabon Italic.

Mastering templates

Many of the documents we create, including letters and invoices, are variations on a theme. They contain many common elements: layout, formatting and often whole chunks of text. Templates save you time and trouble by storing this standard information in a form you can modify again and again.

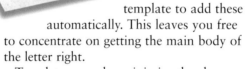

A template is a reusable document containing information that you will use repeatedly in your work. For example, it might be an invoice template in which you have entered all your relevant details, such as a billing number, bank account, company name and address, and so on. So, rather than starting from scratch each time you want to make an invoice, you simply open an existing template, changing or adding only the necessary details.

You will find that templates are invaluable for all sorts of word-processed documents. Even everyday letters benefit: instead of typing your name and address and the date each time you write a letter, you can use a template to add these automatically. This leaves you free to concentrate on getting the main body of the letter right.

Templates can also minimize the chance of making embarrassing typing mistakes: once your template contains the correct information, you can be sure that every document you create based on the template will definitely include exactly the same words. (The time spent checking that the information contained in your templates is correct will be time well spent!)

● Filling in the blanks

Other types of document are also best created as templates for you to fill in the blanks. If you create lots of faxes, for example, which all need boxes for the recipient's name, sender, fax number and date, a template will boost your efficiency.

Templates can include anything you can put into a Word document. If you want a template with special formatting, for example, you can create one with the same typeface and type size changes that you used in the exercise on page 35. On pages 44–47 we'll show you how

There are several useful templates stored ready for use with Word. This is a résumé template – all you have to do is to replace the information with your own.

On pages 44–47 we'll show you how

SHORT CUTS

Often in Word, you will want to select all the text in your document to make a change to it – changing the typeface (font) and its size, for example. Instead of using the Edit menu's Select All command, you can use a keyboard shortcut instead: press [Ctrl]+[A]. You'll immediately see the whole document become highlighted, changing from black text on white to white text on black.

READ-ONLY

Windows can set a file so that you can read it but you can't write any new information to it. This is called a read-only file. If you open a read-only document, you can edit it and add words to it, but you must use the Save As menu option instead of the Save option. This makes sure you save a new file and the original remains intact.

to add simple pictures to your documents and templates. In the exercise below, you'll also see that Word has ready-made templates that include lines, boxes and multiple columns. Documents such as fax cover sheets often incorporate such layout techniques.

● **Template names**
Template names always end in '.dot', so that you can distinguish them from normal Word documents. Because a template is intended to serve as a model for similar documents, Word does not allow you to alter it by saving it in the normal way. These files are read-only documents. When you use a Word template as the basis for a new document, you can only save it as a '.doc' file. The original template remains unaltered.

If you often add lists of items or objects to your documents, try using Word's automatic bullet point button (right) to create them. It's easy to use and creates a properly formatted list with indents (below). Just select the

lines of text you want made into a list, and click once on the button. Word will do it all automatically in an instant. (Note: the button just to the left of the Bullets button produces a numbered list.)

Opening a template in Word

Word's ready-made templates help you get a head start in creating attractive documents. Here's how to do it.

1 Open Word (see page 31), move the mouse pointer to the Menu bar and click once on File. From the drop-down list of commands, click on New.

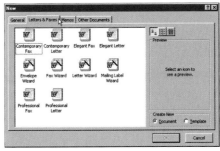

2 The New dialog box appears. Move the mouse pointer along the top of the box to the second category from the left – Letters & Faxes – and click once to see the ready-made templates available.

3 Move the pointer over the 'Contemporary Fax.dot' template and click once with the left button. You will see a preview of the template on the right side of the dialog box.

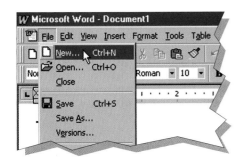

4 While the small preview helps you get an idea of the template and its style, there's no substitute for looking at it full size. Click the OK button to load a new document based on the template into Word for editing.

5 Notice that this fax template contains all the normal fax headings such as 'To:' and 'From:' and dummy text for you to replace. There is also a high level of formatting, with text at different sizes and in various typefaces.

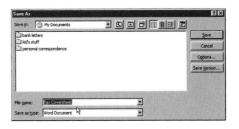

6 Experiment with the template: change some of the text, and then click on Save from the File menu. Notice that you have the Save As dialog box and Word has suggested 'Fax Coversheet.doc' as the file name – the original 'Contemporary Fax.dot' remains unchanged because templates are read-only files.

Creating a new template

If you can't find a suitable template from those supplied with Word, you can create your own from scratch. It's as easy as creating a normal document.

1 To create a new template, click on the File menu and then click on New. You'll see this dialog box.

Click on the Blank Document icon once, then select Template from the Create New section at the bottom right of the box. Click the OK button.

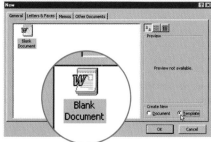

2 You now have a blank template document open on screen. To start, just type in your name and address. Then select these lines of text and click on the Align Right button on the toolbar to move it to the right side of the page.

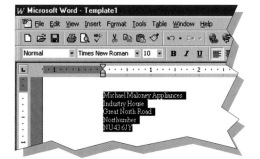

3 Now change the font for the name and address part of your letterhead: with the text selected use the drop-down font menu to choose a new font. Scroll down to find one you like, and then click once on it.

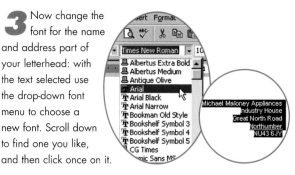

4 Change the size of your address text by using the drop-down font size list. Try sizes between 14 and 20. Do experiment – try choosing fonts and sizes that give your letterhead different types of character: businesslike, informal, etc.

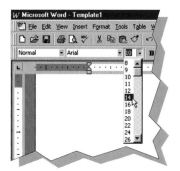

5 To insert the date without having to type it in by hand, choose Date and Time from the Insert menu. A small dialog box pops up that lets you select the date and time format.

Word can supply many different formats at the click of a mouse button. Use the scroll bar to move through them, then click on the one you want.

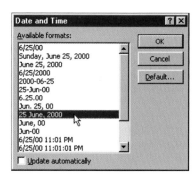

6 Below the main list of formats, you will notice a small check box, labeled Update automatically.

If there is no check mark in this box, click once on it to make one appear. Click on the OK button to return to the template.

7 Today's date now appears in your document, at the position of the text insertion point. Every time you use this template to create a new document, Word will insert the correct date. Like all other parts of your template, you can change the appearance of the date – font, size, etc. – with the normal menu options and tools. The documents you create from this template will reflect this.

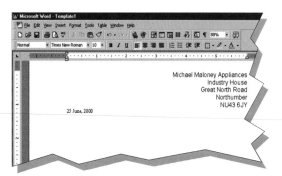

8 Now add a subject line to the document. Press the [Enter] key three times to create some space after the date line. Then type in a subject. If you find you often create letters with the same subjects over and over again, you can make a template for each to save more time when you write the letters. Remember to name them appropriately so that you use the right one.

9 Center the subject line by selecting the line and clicking once on the Center button on Word's Formatting toolbar. You can also underline the words, if you wish.

10 With the line still selected, use the mouse to make the subject bold (click the B button on the toolbar). The line will change from plain to bold text.

Microsoft® Word

11 All that remains is to add a salutation and a closing. Underneath the subject line, insert a blank line then a 'Dear Sir or Madam' line. If it appears centered in your document, use the Align Left button to correct it.

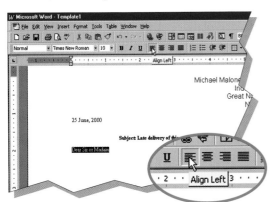

12 Leave a few blank lines under the salutation – this is where you'll add the main body of your letters when you use the template. Now type a closing, including your name with space for a signature.

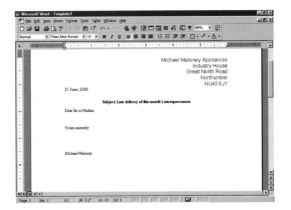

13 Now it's time to save your letterhead template for future use. Move the mouse pointer to the File menu, click once and then click on the Save As option.

GRAYED-OUT MENU ITEMS

As you use the menus and options in Word, you'll often come across menus and options that you can read, but not select. These entries have gray text instead of the usual black.

The grayed-out menu items indicate operations that cannot be performed at the current time. In this case (below), we've just started Word right after starting Windows. Before typing anything, we've clicked on the Edit menu.

Notice that most of the options are grayed-out. Think about them for a moment and you can see how this makes sense. You cannot Copy or Cut anything from the document because there is

nothing selected. Likewise, you cannot Paste anything into the document because there's nothing in the Clipboard (Windows has just started, so the Clipboard is empty).

14 A dialog box appears, and Word suggests a name based on the first line of text in the template. Notice that the Save As type line is grayed out – you can only save this file as a .dot (template) file.

15 Now choose New from the File menu, and you'll see your new template icon ready to use next to the Blank Document icon (the template Word normally uses). Click on the icon for your template and press the OK button.

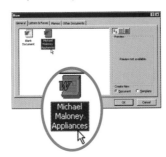

16 A new document will open, ready for you to fill in the blanks. You can go straight to the main body of your letter and type the important parts, confident that the other parts are exactly as you entered them into the template. Notice that the date also changes to show today's date.

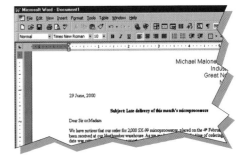

How to work faster with Word

Whether you are working with long documents or lots of short letters, Word has several tricks up its sleeve to help you get through your work more efficiently. Here's how to boost your speed skills.

Most PC users spend a lot of their time using their word processor. Because it's the most popular piece of software, the software's programmers have added many shortcuts and special tools to help you make more effective use of your time.

Here, we'll cover some of the tricks in Word's repertoire that you might not have spotted yet, which can help you work faster and smarter in Word.

● Cut, copy and paste
We've already seen how the Cut, Copy and Paste commands found in the Edit menu are extremely useful tools (see pages 16–17). For Word users, it gets even better – Word can use drag and drop (see pages 14–15) to move parts of your document as quickly as you can use the mouse.

These techniques are probably the most effective skills a Word user can have. See the box below for a step-by-step guide.

● Page control and previewing
We shall also introduce some powerful ways in which to manage how your documents look on paper. And we'll show you how to avoid guesswork when it comes to printing.

Word processors have many built-in features – activated by your keyboard and mouse – which can help you complete routine tasks more quickly.

COPY AND PASTE VERSUS DRAG AND DROP

Copying and pasting in Word work just like they do in other Windows programs (see pages 16–17). You select the words or paragraphs you want to copy or move, copy them into the Windows Clipboard and paste them in the new position.

Alternatively, you can use the drag and drop technique we covered on pages 14–15 to copy and move text in Word. As with all drag and drop techniques, you start by selecting the text you want to copy. This lets Word know what text you want to move.

Once your text is highlighted, move the mouse pointer over it and click and hold down the left mouse button. Now move the mouse down; you will see the pointer change to show a special symbol (a rectangle, right), which indicates that Word has 'picked up' the selected text.

Move the pointer to the position where you want to place the text and let go of the mouse button. The text moves as soon as you release it.

Select some text in your letter or document, click on Edit in the Menu bar and click on the Copy command from the drop-down list.

Move the text insertion point to the position you'd like the copied text to go and then select the Paste command from the Edit menu.

Starting on a new page

As you type, Word will add a page break when you fill each page. For more precise control over the appearance of your documents, you can also add your own breaks.

WHAT IT MEANS

MARGINS

Margins are the white spaces that surround the printed area of the documents you create in Word and other programs. By default (automatically), you will get a white border of about an inch (2.5 cm) on each of the four sides of your pages. We'll show you how to change the size of these margins later in the course.

IF YOU HAVE typed long documents in Word, you will have noticed that every so often the program automatically inserts a dotted line right across the Word window. You will probably also have noticed that when you print your documents there is no such dotted line across the page.

In fact, the dotted line appears exactly at the position where one page finishes and another starts. The dotted line is there to show you when you've reached the bottom of a page. It is Word's visual reminder of the boundary between pages, and is called a page break.

If you experiment by adding lines of text to a page, you'll notice that the dotted line moves. Word automatically calculates the number of lines you can have on a page. This figure depends on the paper size, the margins and the size of your text.

● **Automatic or manual?**

The trouble with Word's automatic page breaks is that sometimes you will want to deliberately start a new page – for example, to begin a new chapter or section of a document. So how can you put a page break exactly where you want it?

Word gives you the power to do this by inserting a manual page break, a code that tells Word that no matter how many text lines there are on the current page, you would like the next line to start on a new page.

Like automatic page breaks, the manual page break appears as a dotted line across the window, but with the words 'Page Break' to remind you that it's a fixed page break. If you want to remove a manual page break, you just delete it. Put the text insertion point on the line and press the [Del] key.

Inserting a manual page break

You don't have to accept the page breaks Word automatically gives you, nor do you have to insert lots of blank lines just to move onto the next page. Here's how to get full control of your page breaks.

1 To insert a manual page break at any position in the document, first move the text insertion point to the position you want the new page to start (you can use the mouse or the cursor keys to do this).

Click on the Insert menu and then click on Break from the list of commands.

2 The Break dialog box pops up in the middle of your Word window. Make sure Page break is selected (it should have a black dot in the small white circle; if it doesn't, click on the circle). Click on the OK button to return to your document.

SHORT CUTS

There's a quick way to insert a page break straight from the keyboard. If you press [Ctrl]+[Enter] you will see a dotted page break line appear at the position of the text insertion point.

3 After the dialog box closes, you will see a dotted line across the document with the words 'Page Break' centered in it. This serves to remind you that this break is one that you have created rather than an automatic one added by Word.

4 New text appears right after the dotted line – it will be the first thing printed on that page. This is very useful for creating pages where you need only a small amount of text at the top of each page. It's much better than adding lots of blank lines to push text onto new pages.

Previewing before printing

It's not always easy to visualize how your document will look when you print. So here's how you can get Word to let you check your document before you waste your paper.

WHEN YOU take a lot of effort to prepare a lengthy word-processed document, it's all too easy to lose sight of how it will actually look when you print it on paper. If you print the document without checking, you could end up wasting a lot of time redoing something that

doesn't quite look as you expected it to.

To avoid this pitfall, Word provides a print preview tool. This shows you on the screen what your document will look like on paper without you having to actually print it.

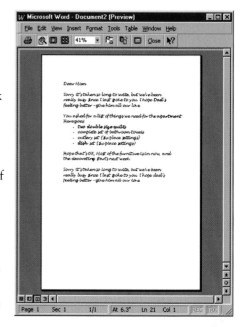

Use Word's print preview feature to check that your letters and documents look right before committing them to paper.

PC TIPS

The best way to get an idea of how your document will really look on paper is to switch to a different view while you type. Usually, Word shows your document in what it calls a Normal view. This shows what the text looks like, but doesn't give a precise representation of actual pages and doesn't depict how the margins look in the final version. You can see a more accurate view of the document by switching to the Page Layout view.

To do this, select Page Layout from the View menu. Like Print Preview, Page Layout view lets you see exactly what each page of your document will look like when printed. The big bonus is that with the Page Layout view you can work directly on your document and adjust the position of objects. You can see instantly how your changes will affect the printed version of your document. You may wonder why anyone works with the Normal view. After all, it's less accurate than Page Layout view. Usually the reason is that on some computers editing a document in Normal view is significantly quicker than in Page Layout view.

● **Saving paper**
If you can get into the habit of using the preview before you print each document, you'll save yourself lots of paper. In particular, it's very useful for catching those instances when a single line carries over from one page onto another.

When you catch this problem through the preview, you can go back to the document and correct the cause.

You can get to the print preview tool by selecting Print Preview from the File menu. When you do this, all the normal toolbars at the top of the Word window will be replaced by just one toolbar and the main editing area of the screen will display a picture of the whole current page (above right).

You'll notice that the mouse pointer changes to a small magnifying glass with a '+' sign inside it (right). This indicates that you can click to zoom in and see a close-up view. Once you have zoomed in, the pointer changes to show a '–' sign; click with this pointer and you'll zoom back out again.

● **Page by page**
If your document has several pages, Word will display the page you were working on when you chose Print Preview. Use the [Page Down] and [Page Up] keys (or use the scroll bars) to move from page to page to see the rest of the document.

If you spot a problem, click the Close button to go back to your document and make any changes. Of course, once you're happy with what you see in the print preview, you can print your document by clicking on the Print button at the far left of the toolbar.

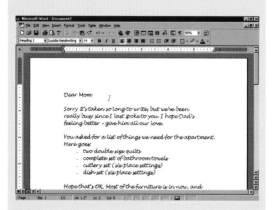

Page Layout view lets you see how each page of your document would look when printed and allows you to edit it.

SHORTCUTS

You can quickly close the print preview window and go back to your document to make changes to it, simply by pressing the [Esc] key.

PC TIPS

At the bottom of Word's right scroll bar, you will see these three small buttons. The two double-arrowhead buttons work like page turners – quickly moving to the top of the page before or after the one you are currently working on. The middle button is used for moving between different objects in a document. We'll show you how to get the most from this button later in the course.

Scrolling around your documents

The longer your Word document becomes, the more difficult it is to find your way around it. Here are our tips for hassle-free document navigation.

MOST DOCUMENTS are too big to fit on the screen all at once. Scrolling is the basic Windows technique you can use to move backward and forward through a document so that its other parts are displayed on screen. The easiest way to scroll through a Word document is to use the scroll bar down the right side of the window.

All you have to do is press the button at the bottom of the scroll bar with a down arrow on it to move forward through your document. If you want to move backward, press the button at the top of the scroll bar with an up arrow on it.

There is another scroll bar along the bottom of the Word window so that you can move sideways in wide documents.

● Drag and drop scrolling

The alternative is to drag and drop the slider button inside the scroll bar. This has the added advantage that Word tells you where you are in the document through the pop-up yellow page number box (see right).

Practice scrolling – it's a lot quicker than using the cursor keys to move through a document one line at a time. You'll also find that it is a useful technique throughout Windows.

Two views on one document

Sometimes it is useful to be able to look at two different parts of the same document. If scrolling back and forth is too tiresome, here's the tip that solves the problem.

1 Move the mouse pointer to the thin button right at the top of the scroll bar. You will see it change from the usual pointer shape to a special double-headed arrow. The arrows indicate which directions you can drag the button.

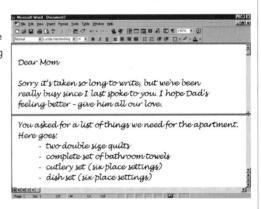

2 Click on the scroll bar button, then, keeping the left mouse button pressed, drag it down the screen. As you do, you'll see that the pointer drags a thick gray line down through your document. Drop the line halfway down your screen.

3 As soon as you drop the line, you'll see that the button expands horizontally to become a divider that fits across the Word window. This divider splits the single Word window into two independent panes, each with its own scroll bars.

4 To work with two views on the same document, just use the scroll bars so that each pane shows one of the areas that you are interested in. Drag the scroll bar with the mouse as usual (the small yellow page indicator can help you locate particular pages on your longer documents).

When you no longer require two panes to view your document, simply drag the divider bar back up to the top of the scroll bar. When you let go, it will revert to its small, thin-button state on the right-hand side.

Adding pictures and special effects to documents

They say that a picture paints a thousand words, so it's good to know that Word lets you insert pictures to liven up your letters. Here's our guide to spicing up your documents.

So far we've used Word for the bread-and-butter job of manipulating text. However, the most interesting documents use special effects and pictures to liven up plain text that might otherwise look boring.

Word has the tools to help you create a thrilling party invitation just as easily as you can write a sober business letter. But it isn't just fun documents that benefit from jazzing up – pictures and text effects can help reinforce the serious messages you might want to convey in your business documents.

● More ways to add style

We've already seen how altering text size, emphasis and typeface can change the appearance of your letters. Now we'll see that Word has another trick up its sleeve for really exciting text effects: the WordArt tool.

You can use WordArt to type in any word or phrase and then stretch and squeeze it in many more ways than you can with normal text. For example, you can rotate WordArt text to any angle, give its letters outlines in one color and fill their insides with a different one, or distort text by changing its height and width. You can also decide how the normal text in your document will wrap around the special text objects you create with WordArt. You can even choose to make the text run along curves and wavy lines. WordArt is an easy tool to master and you can create some really stunning effects with just a little practice and experimentation.

Stretch your words to any shape you want with WordArt.

● Adding pictures

Word also gives you a simple way to add pictures to your documents and letters. You can use pictures supplied as part of the Word software package, or graphics you have created in Microsoft Paint or another graphics program. Adding photographs is equally easy.

As with the text in WordArt, once you've inserted a picture you can manipulate it in many ways. For instance, you can move the picture in the document, change its size and distort its shape. You can also decide how the text in your document will wrap around the picture, and you can change the colors in it by altering brightness and contrast.

There's no reason why you need to put up with lifeless text-only letters. Add some sparkle to your documents with the following step-by-step guides.

Many documents are much more attractive when you add pictures and special effects.

WHAT IT MEANS

WRAP

Place an object into your document, and text runs – or wraps – around it. Photos usually have a square (or regular) wrap. The hands stretching the balloon on this page look better with a wrap that follows their shape (irregular wrap).

Using WordArt to create a party invitation

WordArt is an easy and fun way to be more creative with your PC. If plain text just won't do for your documents, here's how to give them a new lease on life.

1 Let's see how you can use Word's WordArt tool to create special text effects to liven up a party invitation. First, you'll need to type in and format the text for your invitation. Here we've typed the main part of the text in 12pt Times New Roman with some text aligned left and some aligned right.

2 To create a piece of WordArt, click on the Insert menu, click on the Picture option from the drop-down list of commands and then click on WordArt.

3 The dialog box you now see (left) shows simple previews of the WordArt styles available. There are plenty to choose from; choose an appropriate one and click on the OK button. Now you'll see the dialog box where you can type in your text (right). Simply type a phrase such as 'Come To My Party!', choose 40pt as the size and select a typeface from the list box – we've picked Impact. When you click on the OK button, WordArt will apply the style of your choice to the words you've typed in.

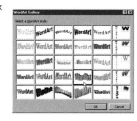

4 You will see the text appear in your document. Look closely and you'll see small 'handles', some white, some yellow. Use the white handles to resize the text, and use the yellow diamond handles to change the waviness and angle of the text – experiment to see how they work.

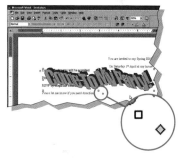

5 There's a special WordArt toolbar (below) to customize your heading further. We want our text to wrap around the WordArt object. Click on the Format WordArt button (fourth from the left on the toolbar) to see the formatting dialog box (right). Click the Wrapping tab, select the Top & bottom option and click on the OK button.

6 Click on the Free Rotate button in the toolbar (fifth from the right in the WordArt toolbar) and you'll see four green circular handles at the corners of the text.

Use the mouse to drag the handles; as you do, you'll see an outline of your WordArt object rotate. Let go and you'll see the object redraw. Click on the button again when you've finished.

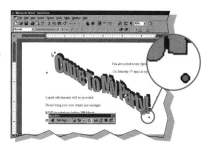

7 Experiment with the other effects on the toolbar. Here, we've clicked on the WordArt Same Letter Heights button, fourth from the right (inset), which stretches lowercase letters to the same height as capital letters. You can change the colors of the text using the Colors and Lines tab of the Format WordArt dialog box (see step 5).

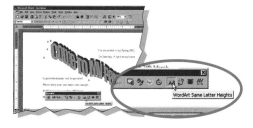

8 You can change the position of the WordArt object in your document by dragging and dropping it. You'll notice that as your mouse passes over the object, it changes to a four-headed arrow to show that you can move it around in your document. Notice that because we selected a top and bottom wrap for the object, the document text reflows around it each time we move it.

9 Why don't you try another special effect? The button on the extreme right controls how close together the text characters appear. We've shown the effect of the tight character spacing option in our example.

Adding graphics with clip art

To add character to your documents, why not insert a picture? You'll find that a great selection of ready-to-use illustrations is supplied with your Word software.

1 We've started another invitation – this time to a children's party – to show how to add clip art. Type in some text for your invitation then click on the Insert menu, select Picture and then choose **Clip Art** from the options.

2 The Microsoft Clip Gallery shows you the picture categories available. Pull down the slider at the right of the window to see the categories and then click once on a category to see what images it contains.

3 Scroll down the window that appears to see the category's images. Choose a picture and click on it: a small menu bar appears to its right; click on the first icon in the bar to insert the image in your document.

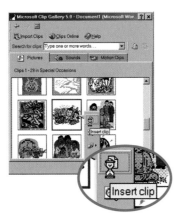

4 The picture appears immediately in your invitation. If you need to move it in your document, you can drag and drop it to another position. When the mouse pointer is over the image, it changes to a four-headed arrow to show the picture can be moved in this way.

5 The picture has eight white boxes at its corners and along the sides. These are handles, and they allow you to change the picture's size. Click on the top-left one and drag it down to the right; as you do so, a dotted line appears to indicate the new size. Release the button and the picture resizes itself.

6 The picture has its own toolbar, which appears automatically. The buttons help you to adjust the appearance of the picture in your document. Hold the mouse pointer over the buttons and an explanation will pop up. Try out the tools to see their effects. The button on the far right undoes any changes and returns the picture to its original state.

7 Click on the second button from the left – the Image Control button. Choose Watermark from the pop-up list. The picture now appears almost transparent. You can use this command, together with the Brightness and Contrast buttons, to adjust the appearance of the picture in your document.

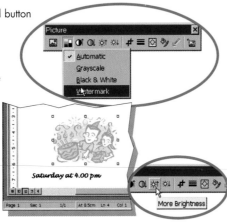

8 If you decide you don't like this picture, double-click on it and the Clip Gallery will reappear. Click on the Keep Looking link at the bottom of the window to display more pictures. The number and type of pictures you will see depends on how your Word software was installed. (Your Word software CD-ROM contains a whole folder of clip art.) If you are connected to the Internet, click on the Clips Online button to go to Microsoft's clip art Web site.

Inserting your own graphics to create a unique letterhead

For the ultimate in personalization, you can use pictures created in programs such as Paint to illustrate and decorate your Word letters.

Letterheads really benefit from the custom-made look. Create your own distinctive logo and insert it into your letters.

YOU'VE SEEN how you can add text effects and clip art graphics to your Word documents. But there will always be occasions when you can't quite find the right piece of clip art for a particular document. If this is the case, the only thing to do is create the image in a graphics program and insert it into your Word letter. This way you can create exactly the picture you want and make your documents stand out from those made with standard clip art.

We'll show you how to create your own pictures using Paint on pages 62–63. In the meantime you can use any bitmap in the following step-by-step guide.

● **Adding a logo**

One example of how to use your own drawings is to create your own letterhead to make your letters more attractive and individual. Try different types of logos before choosing one.

As with WordArt and clip art graphics, Word gives you plenty of control over how your own pictures appear in documents. In fact, you can do everything to your drawing that you can do to a piece of clip art. You can position your drawings precisely, change shape and size, and specify how text should wrap around them.

Adding a logo from Paint to a Word document

If you can insert clip art into your Word documents, you'll find that it's just as easy to add pictures you've created yourself to a document. Here we make an attractive, customized letterhead.

1 To start off our letterhead, we've typed some typical name, address and contact details at the top of our page. Then we've clicked on the Insert menu, the Picture command and then the From File option.

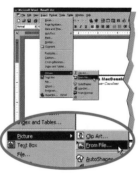

2 To insert a logo created in Paint, click on the Look in: box and select the (C:) drive. Select a folder containing a Paint file – we are using the 'logo.bmp' file. Click on it to see a preview in the space to the right. Press the Insert button. (See pages 62–63 for details on how to create a logo in Paint.)

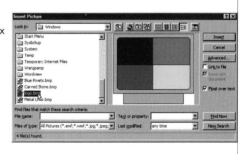

3 Don't worry if your text has wrapped oddly around the logo: click the Text Wrapping button and choose the None option from the drop-down list of commands.

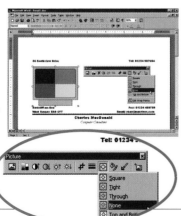

4 Use the handles on the logo's edges to make it smaller, then drag it to the top of the page. Depending on your logo and the information in your letterhead, other layouts may work better. Once you are happy with your letterhead, save it as a template (see pages 36–39). That way you can use it whenever you write a letter.

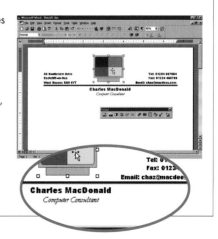

Spreadsheets made easy

Confused by the very idea of a spreadsheet? Not even sure what a spreadsheet is? Here's a straightforward introduction to one of the most useful PC programs.

If you thought spreadsheets were only for accountants and other number crunchers, think again. Today's spreadsheets are so flexible even home PC users can use them to tackle any number of domestic chores, such as tracking your bank balance, working out expense claims and even helping with schoolwork.

You can do so much with a spreadsheet that it is hard to explain with a single example. Unlike a word processor, which is like an advanced typewriter, the spreadsheet has no simple equivalent. Instead, it is a unique and powerful combination of different tools.

To start with, a spreadsheet is stuffed full with the math capabilities of an advanced calculator, but even better, it can also make

stunning graphs with a few mouse clicks. It is laid out in a table of rows and columns so it looks a little like an accountant's ledger book. But unlike a book, you can add new rows and columns as it suits you, without tearing the whole thing up and starting from scratch.

Best of all, if you want to see the effect that a change in one of the numbers you have entered has on the rest, you need only alter a single number and the spreadsheet will perform the calculations for you.

● Rows and columns

Much like the grid you use when you're playing the children's game Battleships, each column of the spreadsheet has a letter heading (A, B, C, ...) and each row is

Getting comfortable with a few simple spreadsheet functions could revolutionize the way you handle your home finances.

WHAT IT MEANS

CELL

The cell is the basic building block of the spreadsheet. Each cell can contain numbers, words or even dates.

numbered (1, 2, 3, ...). You can refer to each and every cell in the table by using its column-row coordinates: A1, A2, B5 or G12, for example.

The trick that lets a spreadsheet work its magic is being able to use figures in one cell of the table in calculations in other cells. For example, if you want cell A1 to show

the contents of cell A2 plus the contents of cell A3, you would simply type '=A2+A3' into cell A1. You can add, subtract, divide, multiply and perform many other functions in spreadsheet calculations.

Don't panic if this sounds like algebra. We'll take you step-by-step through all the varied spreadsheet uses and you'll soon wonder how you ever managed without one.

The spreadsheet – your flexible friend

From adding up your shopping bills to keeping track of all your domestic finances, spreadsheets are designed to help you sail through even the most confusing numerical and financial tasks.

Here's a spreadsheet at its simplest: a shopping list with one column (A) used for the type of item and another (B) for its price. At the bottom, there's a row for the total, and Excel calculates the total figure (in B11) by adding up all the figures in cells B2 to B10.

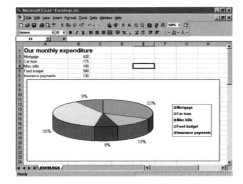

Sometimes looking at numbers in a graphic form can really help them make sense. Here Excel shows the domestic expenditure figures entered in column B as a pie chart. It's easy to see at a glance where the biggest slice of the family budget is going.

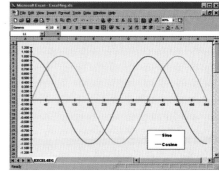

Spreadsheets can also help give a better understanding of math – great for school-children and adults alike. A spreadsheet's ability to show instant results in a graph without resorting to old-fashioned pencil and paper plotting encourages experimentation.

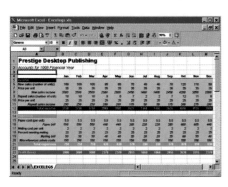

For the self-employed home PC user, a spreadsheet can be vital. Here you can see monthly income and expenses. What happens if the price of paper goes up? Just type in the new price, and you will instantly see the effect on profitability. These 'what-if' calculations are a spreadsheet's strongest feature.

You don't have to use any calculations in your spreadsheet. Some people find that its ready-made table layout (above) makes it ideal for keeping simple lists. Here we've shown a list of contacts, one per row, with columns for names, addresses, telephone numbers etc.

A spreadsheet doesn't always have to look like a grid. We've taken the same information from the previous example and asked Excel to show it in a form (below). Here you see one row of data at a time, and just click through the list.

The Excel worksheet

Worksheets are the documents that Excel uses to store and display information. Built from a grid of rows and columns, a worksheet is easy to understand once you know the basics. Get started with our step-by-step guide.

Toolbars
Excel's toolbars provide one-click access to many common commands.

Name box
The Name box displays the coordinates of the current cell.

Current cell
The current cell is indicated by the black highlight around it.

Rows
Rows in the worksheet are identified by number.

Worksheet tab
Excel documents can contain many worksheets. You click on a tab to select each one.

Status bar
Most of the time, you'll see 'Ready' here, indicating that Excel is waiting for you to input information. Even when it's working on huge calculations, Excel rarely keeps you waiting.

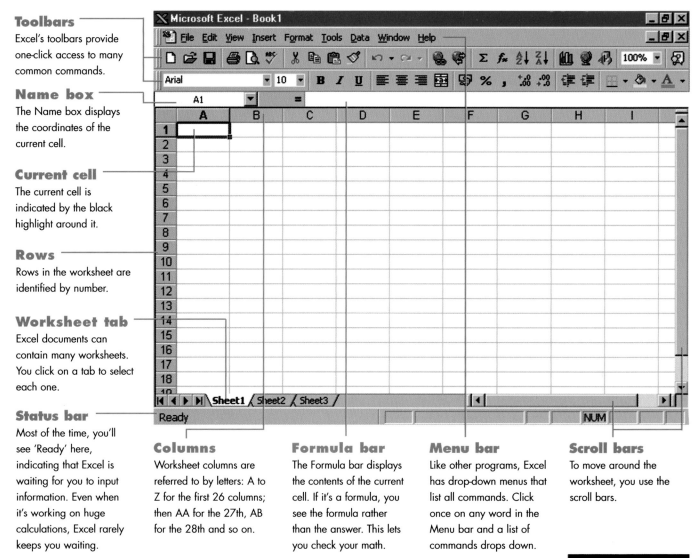

Columns
Worksheet columns are referred to by letters: A to Z for the first 26 columns; then AA for the 27th, AB for the 28th and so on.

Formula bar
The Formula bar displays the contents of the current cell. If it's a formula, you see the formula rather than the answer. This lets you check your math.

Menu bar
Like other programs, Excel has drop-down menus that list all commands. Click once on any word in the Menu bar and a list of commands drops down.

Scroll bars
To move around the worksheet, you use the scroll bars.

When you first start up the Excel spreadsheet, you'll notice that a grid of rectangles (or cells, as they're known) occupies most of the window. This grid is called a worksheet and an Excel document can have as many worksheets as you need.

To start Excel, click on the Windows Start button, click Programs on the pop-up menu and Microsoft Excel from the program list. You'll see a screen like the one above.

An Excel worksheet can have up to 256 columns and 16,384 rows – that's more than enough for any home PC user! Rows are numbered from 1 to 16,384 and columns are labelled from A to Z, then AA to AZ, BA to BZ, and so on. A cell can contain almost any kind of information: text, numbers or a formula.

Entering information is easy: click on a cell and type in whatever you want. As you type, you'll see the line of information appear in the cell. Once you've finished typing in that

S H O R T C U T S

To move quickly back to the first cell of a worksheet, A1, press [Ctrl]+[Home]. The [Home] key is to the right and a little higher than the [Enter] key.

cell, press the [Tab] key to move to the cell to the right or press [Enter] to move to the cell below. If you notice a mistake after you've moved to a new cell, you can click on the cell and type in all the information again. A more useful way to correct mistakes is by using the

Formula bar: click on a cell and the Formula bar shows its contents, click on the information in the Formula bar and you can correct the part that's wrong. Press [Enter] when you've finished. This is often much quicker than having to retype the whole cell.

Adding up with Excel

The best way to gain confidence with worksheets is to use one. Let's start with a simple example – your supermarket bill. You can type in all the items and their prices and get Excel to add up the total for you.

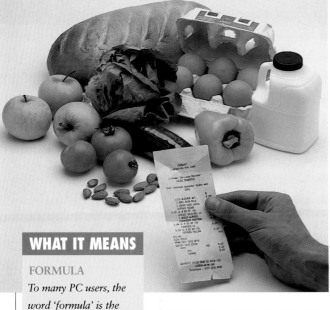

WHAT IT MEANS

FORMULA

To many PC users, the word 'formula' is the one thing that makes spreadsheets seem complicated. In fact, it's really just another way of saying calculation.

Here's our tip for success: when you are typing a formula into a cell, it's just like using a calculator, but instead of pressing the equal sign (=) at the end of the calculation, you begin with it.

Calculator:

  number + number =

Worksheet formula:

  = cell + cell

1 We're going to type the names of the items from a supermarket bill into column B and the price of each item into column C. Click on cell B2 to select it and type the word 'Item'. Now select cell C2 and type the word 'Price'. Notice how the cell has a thick black border around it to remind you that it is the one you're working in.

2 Click on cell B3 (located directly below 'Item') to select it and type the word 'Apples'. Now press the [Tab] key to move across to cell C3 (the one located directly below the 'Price' heading). This time type in '1.25' for the price of the apples. Don't bother with the $ sign for now – we'll cover currency fully later in the course.

3 Now keep adding more items and prices in the cells below until you've completed your list. We've included bread at 59¢, wine at $4.49, cheese at $2.21 and a bar of chocolate at 35¢ – your list might be different.

Note: when typing amounts that are less than one dollar, just type them as a decimal. For example, type '.35' for 35¢.

4 Click the cell that's located below the final price you typed into your list (this is cell C8 in our example). Now insert the formula that adds up this list by typing: '=C3+C4+C5+C6+C7'

Then press the [Enter] key and Excel knows you've finished and adds up the figures. It will show the answer in place of the formula.

5 The power of spreadsheets is in their ability do the sum again if something changes. Imagine that you mistyped the price of the wine: it was really $5.29. On a calculator you'd have to start again. In Excel, all you have to do is change the price and it will recalculate the total in a fraction of a second. Try it. Now imagine how useful this is for long lists!

Using Excel formulas

You're not just limited to simple sums with a spreadsheet – if you include other mathematical operations in your formulas, you can make Excel work harder for you and your family. Here's how to forecast your monthly food budget.

If you tried the Excel exercise on page 51, you will already have seen how Excel can save you having to do basic arithmetic. Excel has a whole range of formulas and functions so that it can carry out many more operations for all sorts of home computing tasks.

In the previous exercise, when you added up the right-hand column, you typed in '=C3+C4+C5+C6+C7', which will have been displayed in the Formula bar. All formulas look like this. They always begin with an equal sign (=) to show Excel that it is expected to perform a calculation. Then they contain some cell locations and details of the mathematical operations that you want Excel to carry out. In this case, Excel understands the calculation displayed in the Formula bar as 'add the contents of cells C3, C4, C5, C6 and C7, and put it in the current cell'.

● Summing it up

Excel calculations can be as simple or as complicated as you want, depending on the instructions that you put in. But most of the time, they will just use the four basic arithmetic instructions that appear on a calculator: plus, minus, multiply and divide.

Unlike a calculator, however, once you have entered a formula it will stay in place in the worksheet, and if you change your data, Excel will automatically redo the calculations and tell you the new answer.

● The Formula bar

Any formula that applies to the current cell is displayed in the Formula bar (see page 50). All formulas must begin with an equal sign (=). That's how Excel knows that what follows is a formula (as opposed to a text title, such as 'Items' or 'Price', a number, such as '12' or '8.56378', or a date, such as '12/07/00').

You type the plus sign with the plus [+] key on the main keyboard or the numeric keypad. For minus, you use the hyphen [-] key or the minus [-] key on the numeric keypad.

Your computer keyboard doesn't have true division or multiplication keys, so you use the forward slash key [/] for division and the asterisk [*] key for multiplication.

For example, to divide cell B2 by cell B7, you would type '=B2/B7'. To multiply cell A6 by B6, you would type '=A6*B6'. You can also use the operations in combination, too. For example, '=A2*B2/B3' would multiply A2 by B2 and divide the result by B3.

You can also use these math operations with numbers. For example, to multiply 23 by 35, type '=23*35' straight into an Excel cell. When you press the [Enter] key, you'll get the answer. You can also combine numbers and cell locations; a formula of '=A2*1.25' multiplies the contents of cell A2 by 1.25.

Figure out your shopping bills efficiently with your own made-to-measure worksheet.

If your spreadsheet is very large, it can be quicker to move around it by using the [Page Up] and [Page Down] keys instead of clicking on the scroll bars with the mouse.

Work out your shopping budget

Calculate your month's food expenditure with Excel.

PC TIPS

There are many other useful math operations you can get Excel to do for you. For example, if you wanted to find the square of 213, just type '=213^2' into any cell. (You type the ^ symbol by typing [Shift]+[6].)

When Excel calculates a formula, it applies the same rules that apply in normal math, using parentheses to show which parts of a calculation should be done first, for instance.

Consider this example:
'=(B2-B3)*B4'.
The parentheses indicate that B3 must be subtracted from B2 first, and then the result should be multiplied by B4.

Compare this to:
'=B2-B3*B4'. Here, you would multiply B3 by B4 and then subtract the result from B2. The answer would be very different. Be careful not to omit needed parentheses.

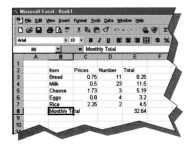

1 Start a new worksheet. We'll use column B to enter the food items and column C for their prices. Click on cell B2 to select it and type in the word 'Item'. Click on cell C2 and type in 'Prices'.

2 Now use column B to enter a range of food items, and column C for the price of each item. Don't bother with the $ or ¢ signs; just type in 75¢ as '.75', and $1.73 as '1.73'.

3 Click on cell D2 and type in 'Number'. In cell D3 type in the number of loaves you buy each month – we've entered '8'. Carry on down the column, adding numbers for each item in your list.

4 Now you can use formulas to enter the calculations you want to perform. Click on cell E2 and type in 'Total'. Then click on cell E3. Type in '=C3*D3' (using the asterisk [*] key). This will multiply the number in C3 by the number in D3.

5 To see how the formula automatically recalculates for you, click on cell C3 and type in a new price: the total in cell E3 will adjust itself. Change the price back, and change the number of loaves in cell C3: again, the total will change.

6 Carry on down column E with these multiplications: in E4, enter the formula '=C4*D4', and so on. Remember: if you make a mistake just retype the cell formula again, or edit the formula on the Formula bar (see page 50).

7 When you reach the bottom of your list, use another formula to work out the total monthly bill. Type 'Monthly Total' into cell B8, then click on cell E8 and type in '=E3+E4+E5+E6+E7'. When you press the [Enter] key, you'll see the overall total. Just like other formulas, any change in prices or numbers will recalculate this figure automatically.

8 You can see how subtraction works by taking the total bill from a monthly shopping budget. Type 'Monthly Budget' in cell B9, click on cell E9 and type a figure for your monthly shopping budget (we have used '125' for $125).

Click on B10 and type in 'Monthly Surplus'. Now click on E10 and enter the formula '=E9–E8'.

9 You do division in a similar way. We will use another formula to work out approximately how much is left over each week from our monthly budget and get Excel to put the result in cell E11.

Click on E11 and type in '=E10/4' (this will divide the contents of cell E10 by 4 – a rough approximation of the weekly surplus).

Selecting cells and moving around in Excel

To make the most of Excel worksheets, you need to know your way around Excel's most important tools. Here's a look at two of the program's most commonly used features.

A t first sight, an Excel worksheet looks fairly daunting, with row upon row and column upon column of cells. However, the cells are nothing more than squares or boxes you might fill in on paper; it all looks very rigid and formal to start with, but you can type information into any box you like.

In the previous exercises, we've shown how Excel can help with simple domestic finances (see pages 51 and 53). Now, we're going to cover two vital Excel principles: how to select cells in the worksheet and how to manage your documents using the File menu.

● Selecting cells
To select a single cell, you can simply move the mouse pointer and click over it. If you want to select a block of cells, hold down the mouse button over a cell at one corner of the block you wish to select. Then, still holding down the mouse button, drag the mouse over the other cells in the block and release the mouse button. The cells in the block will turn black as you drag the mouse over them – this shows they are selected.

Another way to select a block of cells is to click on the cell you want to be at one corner of the block, press and hold down the [Shift] key and click again on the cell you want at the opposite corner of the selection.

● Advanced selection
Both of these techniques select a continuous rectangular group of cells. All the cells must be physically adjacent. Often you'll find, however, that you need to select cells that are not next to each other. How do you select these without selecting all the others in between them?

Luckily, the programmers who made Excel thought of this. You can use the same mouse techniques together with the [Ctrl] key to

Selecting groups of cells that are not next to each other is easy – just use the [Ctrl] key and click on the cells. You'll find that any new cells you click on will be added to the existing selection.

You will find plenty of home computing jobs you can use Excel to tackle.

SHORT CUTS

In addition to using the cursor keys to move from cell to cell, you can also use the [Enter] key. This is useful if you have just used the [Enter] key to finish typing information into a cell. The [Enter] key moves the highlight down one cell position. Use [Shift]+[Enter] to move up one cell.

select any cells you like. Click on the first cell you want to select. Then press and hold down the [Ctrl] key. Now click on all the other cells you want in your selection. Once the [Ctrl] key is pressed down, you can also drag the mouse to add more cells to the selection.

● **Moving around a worksheet**
Excel will also 'remember' your selection if you need to use the scroll bars to move around your worksheet and select yet more cells. Select your first group of cells, use the mouse on the scroll bars until you can see the new cells you want to add, and use the [Ctrl] key technique as before.

When creating a complicated selection, beware of accidentally clicking on a cell without pressing the [Ctrl] key – or you'll have to start over!

PC TIPS

You can select every cell in the worksheet by clicking on the blank button at the top left, where the column and row headings meet. When you click on the button, the whole spreadsheet becomes highlighted. You can now carry out the same operations on the whole worksheet as you would on individual cells, such as changing the typeface.

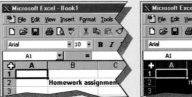

A look down Excel's File menu

In Excel's File menu you will find the commands that allow you to open and save worksheets, and many other useful tools, too; the most common ones have shortcut key commands shown alongside.

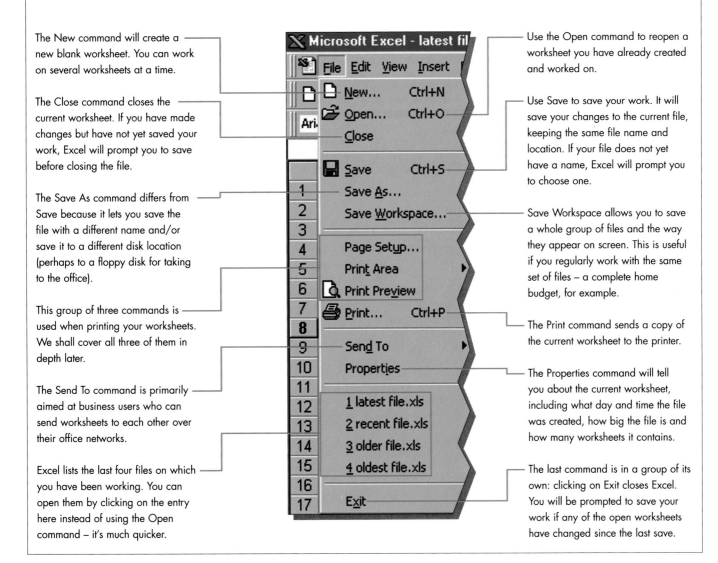

The New command will create a new blank worksheet. You can work on several worksheets at a time.

The Close command closes the current worksheet. If you have made changes but have not yet saved your work, Excel will prompt you to save before closing the file.

The Save As command differs from Save because it lets you save the file with a different name and/or save it to a different disk location (perhaps to a floppy disk for taking to the office).

This group of three commands is used when printing your worksheets. We shall cover all three of them in depth later.

The Send To command is primarily aimed at business users who can send worksheets to each other over their office networks.

Excel lists the last four files on which you have been working. You can open them by clicking on the entry here instead of using the Open command – it's much quicker.

Use the Open command to reopen a worksheet you have already created and worked on.

Use Save to save your work. It will save your changes to the current file, keeping the same file name and location. If your file does not yet have a name, Excel will prompt you to choose one.

Save Workspace allows you to save a whole group of files and the way they appear on screen. This is useful if you regularly work with the same set of files – a complete home budget, for example.

The Print command sends a copy of the current worksheet to the printer.

The Properties command will tell you about the current worksheet, including what day and time the file was created, how big the file is and how many worksheets it contains.

The last command is in a group of its own: clicking on Exit closes Excel. You will be prompted to save your work if any of the open worksheets have changed since the last save.

Styling and coloring your spreadsheets

We've already seen ways to liven up text in Word letters and documents, but you can do the same to your spreadsheets to make them more attractive and easy to read. Here's how to add color and pizzazz to your Excel worksheets.

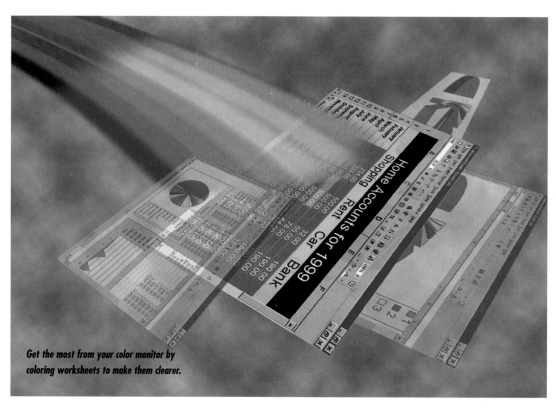

Get the most from your color monitor by coloring worksheets to make them clearer.

In the Word exercises, we've seen how to add spice to a letter (see pages 34–35). This makes it more pleasing to the eye and helps get the right message across. The same principles apply to Excel – indeed, many would argue that the standard white cells crammed with black figures are in desperate need of livening up!

Excel tries to guess how you want the information in your worksheet laid out: it aligns words to the left, and numbers to the right. However, if you want something fancier, then you must do it yourself. It's easy to do, and worth the effort.

The second of Excel's toolbars provides point-and-click access to most of the popular cell formatting commands. Some tools are similar to those of Word; others are specific to Excel. Pause with the mouse over each tool to get a quick description of what it does.

As we've seen in Word, formatting text is easy. You can change the alignment, size, typeface and weight of words and numbers. Many of Excel's tools are exactly the same as those in Word (see below). You can also change the height of rows and width of columns to squeeze in more information.

● A touch of color

It's also simple to add color to your worksheet – just highlight the cells you want to change and click on the Fill Color and Font Color tools (the two buttons at the far right of the toolbar).

Changing the filled color of worksheet cells can be used to great effect. Even if you don't have a color printer, just using color on screen can make spreadsheets easier to work with.

Arial ▾ 10 ▾ **B** *I* U ≡ ≡ ≡ ≡ 国 % , .00 .00 ⊞ ▾ ◇ ▾ A ▾
Underline

Adding clarity

Make your worksheets easier to understand and help to get your point across by styling and formatting the text, adding color and resizing cells.

Microsoft® Excel

SHORT CUTS

Excel responds to many of the same shortcuts that other Windows programs do. For instance, to get bold text, you don't need to move your mouse up to the toolbar. First, select the cells in which you want the text to be bold, then press [Ctrl]+[B].

You can also change text to italics by pressing [Ctrl]+[I] and underline text by pressing [Ctrl]+[U]. To reverse any of these actions, just press the same keys again.

1 Here's how a simple record of quarterly bills might look typed straight into Excel. All the information is there, but it's not easy to follow, so let's do something to make it clearer.

2 We want to make sure that the headings for the bills and the quarters of the year are prominent. Select the cells and press the Bold button.

3 Now we can see that some of the text in some of the cells in the B column is obscured by the C column. To increase the width of column B, move the mouse to the border between the B and the C column buttons. Notice that it changes to a double-headed arrow. Click and drag to the right to make the column wider; you'll see a vertical dotted line indicating the new width of the column.

4 Add cell borders to divide the different parts of the table: select the top row of cells and click on the down arrow by the Borders button. Select the thick black bottom border from the choice of borders. Do the same for the bottom row, with the thinner border.

5 Select the headings again and click on the down arrow next to the Font Color tool. A palette of different-colored squares pops up (right). Click over the white one. As you do, you'll notice that your text seems to disappear. It's still there, but you can't see white text on a white background.

6 Now click the down arrow next to the Fill Color tool. Another color palette pops up: click on the bright red one. Notice that your white text is now visible against the darker background.

7 Now color the cells for the other rows in the same way. We've chosen matching colors for the other rows to minimize eyestrain. (Note: when working on very wide tables of information, it's helpful to choose alternating colors for the rows to help you read across the table.)

8 Now select all the number cells. We want to show that these figures represent money by using Excel's Currency tool. It's in the center of the toolbar and its icon shows dollar bills and coins (left). Click on the button and Excel gets the right currency symbol by checking your Windows country settings (we'll discuss these later in the course). It then uses the symbol and adds two decimal places for smaller denominations.

9 Now that we've increased the amount of information in the cells, the cells are looking a little crowded. First we need to select all four columns, C to F, at the same time. To do this, move the mouse over the column C cell, click and hold the button down and then drag the pointer across the other three columns. You'll see the columns become highlighted.

10 Let go of the mouse (the four columns stay highlighted) and use the column dragging technique (step 3). As you drag, you'll see a dotted line (left) that shows how wide your columns will be. Release the mouse and you'll see that Excel widens all four columns at once. Finally, select the quarterly period cells and use the Align Right button to make them sit over the cost figures (above).

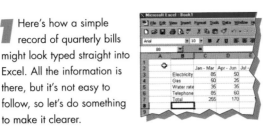

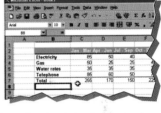
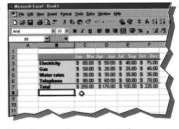
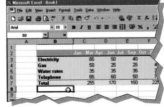

Presenting pie charts

A colorful three-dimensional pie chart is a great way to clearly display the information contained in lists of figures. It can be easy and fun to present your household finances in this pictorial form, so even children will be able to appreciate how the family budget works.

There are few things more daunting than trying to understand what is really happening in a complicated set of figures. Scientists, engineers and business people frequently convert numbers into charts and graphs to make it easier to see at a glance what's going on.

You can borrow this professional technique when you want to analyze the information you store in your spreadsheets at home. What's more, a spreadsheet makes it easy to produce impressive and expert-looking results right away. But the best aspect of using a spreadsheet is that the labor-intensive chore of drawing the graph is taken out of your hands and performed quickly and accurately by your computer.

● **A wizard with numbers**

Excel has a tool called the Chart Wizard that will lead you through a step-by-step process to create a chart or graph from any figures in your spreadsheet. In only a few steps, you can make colorful pie charts, bar graphs or line graphs. For a more artistic touch, you can choose 3D pie charts, cylinders and pyramids.

For any of these charts, you can choose the colors of each part, make notes and add headings. Once you've created your chart, you can position it anywhere you like in a document, resize it or put it on a page of its own. If you decide you don't like the way your chart looks, you can change it by using the Chart toolbar or the Chart menu.

● **Automatic updates**

Perhaps the most powerful feature of charting in Excel is that you don't have to make a new chart every time you change a figure – your chart is dynamically linked to

For the professional touch, Excel can show the 'slices' of a pie chart in three dimensions and a range of different colors.

Pie charts display the family finances clearly enough for everyone to appreciate.

the cells that hold the figures used to create it. In other words, every time you modify one of the cells used in your chart, Excel will automatically redraw the chart to show the effects. Experiment yourself when you've worked through the example opposite. The maroon colored slice of the 3D pie chart in the example represents the $300 mortgage payment. Imagine that there's a change in interest rates and your mortgage repayment goes down to $250.

Click on the cell containing the mortgage figure and type in '250'. Watch to see what happens to the pie chart when you press the [Enter] key. The pie chart is redrawn almost instantly to reflect the change you've just made to the figures.

WHAT IT MEANS

DYNAMICALLY LINKED

If you draw a chart by hand, it's static: if the figures change, the chart stays the same. You must draw the whole thing again. If a chart is dynamically linked, the chart and its figures are permanently related. Just type a new figure and the chart will change immediately to show the effects.

How to create your first pie chart

In this step-by-step example, you'll find out how to use Excel to create a colorful three-dimensional pie chart to show how a typical household budget is sliced up.

PC TIPS

Zoom factor

To change the amount of the worksheet you can see, alter the zoom factor. Look along Excel's top toolbar and toward the right-hand end you'll see a small drop-down list of percentages. Click once to see the drop-down menu of options, or click on the 100% figure in the toolbar to type another number.

1 Type in some figures to represent the major areas of home expenditure, with labels and headings as shown here. We've formatted our table of figures with two colors to make them stand out from the white worksheet (see pages 56–57).

2 Now tell Excel what information you want to include in your pie chart. Select the table by dragging the mouse from the top-left cell to the bottom-right cell. The cells will highlight and look like a negative image. Remember to include the two column headings as well as all the descriptions and amounts, as these will also appear on your pie chart.

3 To chart your information, we'll use Excel's Chart Wizard tool. You start it by clicking on the small graph button toward the right of the toolbar.

4 The first step in the Chart Wizard lets you choose the exact type of chart you want to create. If you click on items in the Chart type list in the column on the left side of the dialog box, the Chart subtypes on the right shows previews of the options available with these types of chart.

Click on Pie in the Chart type list, then click on the picture in the middle of the top row (showing a three-dimensional pie chart) of the Chart subtypes. Then click on Next.

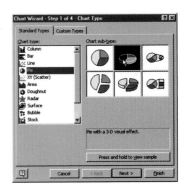

5 On the next screen, tell the Chart Wizard which data you want to use. We've already highlighted the relevant cells (see step 2), so just click Next. Name your chart 'Monthly Expenditure' in the Chart title box and click OK.

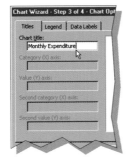

6 Next, the Chart Wizard asks you to choose between showing your pie chart as a completely new worksheet or as a 'floating' object on the page where the table of figures is. Make sure that the As object in: option is selected and click on the Finish button.

7 Excel immediately draws the pie chart on your worksheet. You can make the pie chart larger or smaller by moving the small black handles on the edges of the chart. You can move the whole chart by dragging and dropping it with the mouse pointer.

8 When you click on the pie chart, a Chart toolbar appears. You can modify many aspects of the chart using this, including the colors, the text and the position of any part of it. Click on the drop-down box at the left of the toolbar (below) and select Series "Amount". Now you can pull out a slice of the pie. Click on one of the pie segments to select it; you'll see some small handles appear on its edges. Use the mouse to drag it away from the rest of the pie chart.

You can also change the color of each pie slice by using the Fill Color tool on the Formatting toolbar above the worksheet area (see pages 56–57).

Microsoft® Excel

Adding with AutoSum

We've already seen how easy it is to use Excel to add up a few numbers quickly. Now let's find out the most efficient and accurate way of dealing with much larger sets of figures.

You already know how to use a simple formula to add up a small set of figures, such as a short shopping bill (see pages 50–51). For example, if we wanted to add up the four figures in the first four cells in column C of an Excel spreadsheet, we would use the formula '=C1+C2+C3+C4'. If you put this formula into cell C5, that's where Excel would put the result.

This manual method of typing in the whole formula, including all the cells you want, is fine when you only want to add up a short set of figures, but what happens when you want to add up the contents of 30 or 40 cells? It would be tiresome to type in all the cell names that make up the formula – and you would probably make mistakes along the way. Luckily, Excel includes a tool called AutoSum that takes the hassle out of this chore.

● **Quick and easy**
Here's a simple example of how AutoSum works: let's imagine that you have a column of 20 numbers in cells C1 through C20 and you

want to add them up and put the result in cell C21. First, click on cell C21 to select it and then move up to the Standard toolbar (usually the row of tools directly underneath the menu options). Locate the AutoSum tool (it looks like the capital Greek letter sigma Σ) and click on it. A flashing dotted line will appear around cells C1 through to C20 and a formula like this will appear in cell C21: '=SUM(C1:C20)'. Simply press the [Enter] key to finish the job and the result will appear in cell C21.

● **Watch the gaps**
As you can see, it's quick and easy to do, but you should still take a little care because sometimes Excel has to make guesses about which cells you want to include in your sum.

Let's imagine that there wasn't a number in cell C9 in the previous example. Then Excel would guess that you only wanted to add up the contents of cells C10 through to C20 because of the gap made by the empty C9 cell. Instead of pressing the [Enter] key immediately, you would have to drag and drop with the mouse to select all the cells

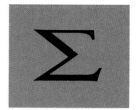

The AutoSum tool, situated in Excel's top toolbar and represented by the Greek letter sigma, is a useful feature when you need to add up a long column of numbers.

between C1 and C20 and then press [Enter].

Excel would make the same sort of guess if cell C9 contained any nonnumerical data. So if there were text, or even another formula in cell C9, Excel would assume that it was the top end of the column of figures you wanted to add up and would only include cells C10 to C20 in its automatic formula.

It's always a good idea to check the total of the entries on your credit card statement – a task that can be achieved easily and accurately by using Excel.

Checking your credit card bill

See how AutoSum can make adding up a list of numbers so easy. Let's use a long number list with which many people are familiar - the credit card bill.

Microsoft® Excel

WHAT IT MEANS

FUNCTION

Excel uses special commands called functions to work out results from data that appear in parentheses after the function. For example, 'SUM(1,2,3)' adds up 1, 2 and 3 to get 6. Excel understands a huge range of functions, including those that work out mathematical problems and calculate statistics.

1 Here's a typical set of monthly credit-card expenses. Open a worksheet and copy the information shown here exactly. We could create a long formula by hand in cell D22 to add them up, but the problem is that there are 18 number entries here and it would be tedious to type in the whole formula.

2 Let's use Excel's AutoSum feature instead. Click on cell D22 and then click on the AutoSum tool (this is the letter Σ in the top toolbar). Excel only selects the cells from D13 onward because it thinks the text in D12 is the top end of the column of figures you want to add up.

3 Press the [Esc] key to cancel the AutoSum. Now change the word 'Fifty' to the number '50' and try again. Click on cell D22 and click the AutoSum tool. This time Excel thinks you want to add up the contents of cells D10 to D21 because cell D9 is empty. It sees an empty cell as the end of a column of figures.

4 You can use the drag and drop technique with your mouse to change the cells automatically selected by Excel. With the dotted outline still showing, click on cell D4, hold down the left mouse button and drag down to select all of the cells from D4 to D21. Release the mouse button when you've finished.

5 Now press the [Enter] key to tell Excel that you've finished selecting the cells. The spreadsheet automatically adds up the column of figures in the cells D4 to D21 and places the result, '829.68', in cell D22. This way is a lot easier than typing in a formula that includes each individual cell!

6 Excel has automatically created the formula in cell D22 for you. Click on this cell and look closely at what comes up in the Formula bar: it says '=SUM(D4:D21)'. Excel has used a special function called SUM to save the effort of including every cell between D4 and D21 in its formula.

7 Now let's go back and fill in the missing amount for the gas. Click on cell D9 and type in '9.50'. Now press the [Enter] key and watch what happens to the total in cell D22. Excel recalculates the sum. Now you know that the horrible truth calculated by the credit-card company is correct!

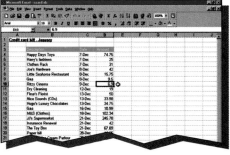

First steps in graphics

The Microsoft Paint program is supplied with Windows. In the following series of tutorials, you'll find out how easy it is to create your own pictures.

Making graphics (or pictures) is one of the most creatively rewarding activities you can do with your computer. You don't even need to buy an expensive graphics program, because Windows already includes an ideal one for beginners, Microsoft Paint.

Apart from being free with Windows, Paint has the great advantage of simplicity. It's the ideal way to come to grips with the basic graphics tools without being bewildered by the vast array of features offered by the more advanced graphics programs.

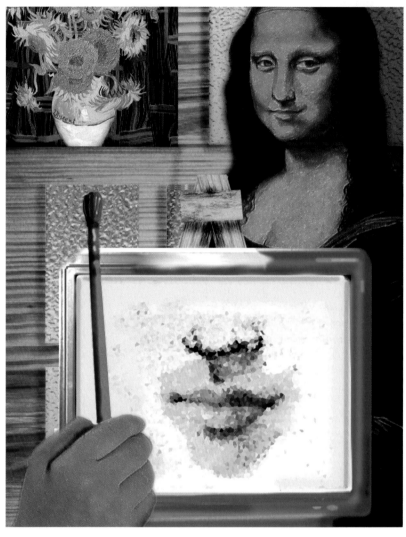

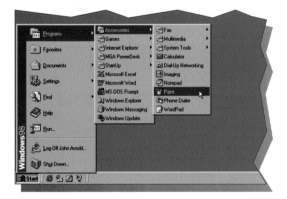

Start Paint by clicking on the Start button, then Programs, then Accessories and then clicking on the Paint option.

A tour around the Paint window

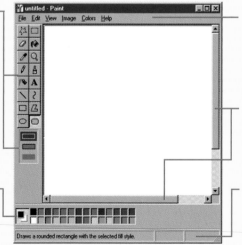

Toolbox
Paint has plenty of tools to use in your pictures. On the opposite page, you get to use the shape-drawing and paint-filling tools.

The lower part of the toolbox changes to give you more options, depending on the tool you chose.

Palette
Just as real painters work with a palette of colors, so does Microsoft Paint.

Menu bar
Paint has six menu items. Click on a word to see the list of commands under each subject heading.

Scroll bars
You can move around a big picture by moving the scroll bars.

Status bar
The bar at the very bottom of the window shows extra information about your picture.

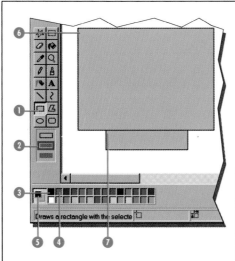

Creating a colored logo

Imagine that a computer consultant friend has asked you to design a new logo for his business. His idea is a computer monitor split into four colorful rectangles. Here's how to paint it on your PC.

❶ Click the toolbox button with the rectangle outline to select the Rectangle drawing tool.

❷ Click on the middle rectangle below the toolbox to choose a filled box with a border.

❸ Select the border color: click on black in the palette with the LEFT mouse button.

❹ Fill the rectangle with color: click on gray in the palette with the RIGHT mouse button.

❺ You will now see a black rectangle on top of a gray one just to the left of the palette.

❻ Now go to the drawing area. Click and keep the left mouse button pressed, and move the pointer across and down the screen until you're happy with the shape, and let go.

❼ Use the mouse to draw another, smaller rectangle underneath the large one, as in step 6. This will represent the monitor stand.

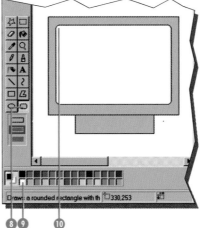

❽ Click on the Rounded Rectangle button at the bottom of the toolbox.

❾ To fill the rectangle with the color white, click on the white box in the palette with the RIGHT mouse button.

❿ Move to the drawing area and draw the screen just inside the gray area, which represents the edge of the monitor.

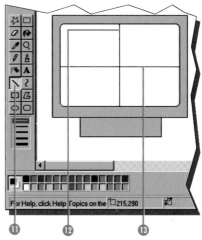

⓫ Select the Line tool.

⓬ Move the pointer to the top of the screen, and draw by holding down the LEFT mouse button as you move the mouse downward.

⓭ Draw a horizontal line across the screen of your monitor picture in the same way.

Press and hold the [Shift] key while drawing the line to keep it perfectly straight.

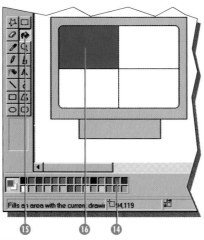

⓮ Click on the blue square in the palette to change the paint color.

⓯ Return to the toolbox and click on the tipping paint can. This Fill tool fills an area of one color with another color.

⓰ Move to the drawing area and click in the white top-left quarter of the screen. This will fill this quarter of the screen with the blue paint you chose in step 14.

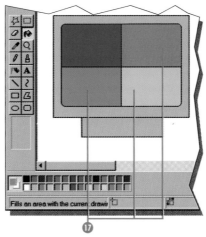

⓱ Now apply other colors to the other three quarters of the monitor screen. You can use the Fill tool as many times as you like – just choose the color from the palette.

If you find paint 'leaks' from one quarter of the screen into another, check for small gaps in the lines you have drawn. Paint will flow through the tiniest of holes. If you find one, draw the line again.

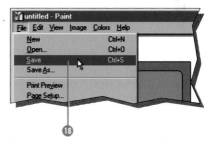

⓲ Now save the picture. Click on the File menu and click on Save.

⓳ Type a name for the picture.

⓴ Click on the Save button.

See page 47 for details of how to add a Paint logo to a letterhead in Word.

Writing with Paint

Graphics programs are perfect for pictures, but some of the best results come when combining pictures and words. Here's how to use Paint's text tricks to enhance your logos and graphics.

Simple doodles, sketches on your computer or formal designs of print quality are easily achievable using a graphics program, such as Microsoft Paint.

We've already seen that Paint provides a wide range of painting tools. An added bonus is that it also gives you the basic tools you need to add words to your pictures. Here we'll show you how to position words exactly where you want them, choose the color and size of the letters and decide the typeface the words appear in.

There are two important tools for controlling the way your text appears: the Text tool and Text toolbar (shown opposite).

Select the Text tool by clicking on the toolbar button marked with a capital A. Move into the painting area and see the pointer change shape and become a cross. Click on the position you want your text to appear in. A rectangular text box appears, containing a flashing text cursor. Type some text into this box. The box gets deeper as you type more text, but not wider. You can widen it by dragging with the mouse. Press and hold the left mouse button on the text box's corner or side squares and move the mouse down and to the right to create a bigger text box.

● **Colorful language**

You can choose the color of the text and its background. At the color palette, use the left mouse button to click on the color for text and use the right mouse button to choose the color for the box. If you don't want a solid background, for example, if you want to put words on top of a picture, make the box's background transparent. Do this by clicking on the lower of the two buttons in the lower section of the Paint toolbar after you click the Text tool.

PC TIPS

multicolor!

Once you have added words to your painting, you can use other Paint tools on them. For example, you can use the Fill tool to color in individual letters after you've placed them in your painting.

Be wary of paint that leaks from letters into the rest of your picture: the fill affects all adjacent areas of the same color.

If the worst happens, and paint does leak out of the letters, you can click on Edit in the Menu bar and then select Undo to remove the effects of your Fill command.

SHORT CUTS

There may be times when you want to paint using the maximum possible area of the screen. Press [Ctrl]+[A] and [Ctrl]+[T] to remove the color palette and toolbar and you now have almost the whole screen area for painting. Whenever you want to see the palette and toolbar again, just press the same keyboard shortcuts to bring them back into view.

Adding text to a painting

In the exercise on page 63, we created a colorful logo for a computer consultant. Here's how to use Paint's built-in text capabilities to add name and contact details to the painting to simulate a business card layout.

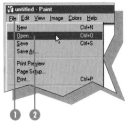

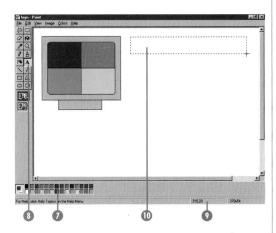

We'll start by opening the computer screen logo we created in the last exercise (see page 63).

1 Click on the word File on the Menu bar.

2 Click on Open.

The Open dialog box is very similar to the Save dialog box.

3 Use the scroll bars until you can see the 'logo' file.

4 Click on 'logo'.

5 Click on the Open button. After a moment, your logo appears in the Paint window.

6 Maximize the Paint window to fill the screen. You can then see and use the area to the side of the logo.

7 Choose a color for your text from the palette.

8 Click on the Text tool (shown by the letter A).

9 This panel shows the **pixel** coordinates of your pointer change as you move it around the painting area.

10 Click and drag an area for the first text line, making a note of the first number (the X coordinate) in the panel.

WHAT IT MEANS

PIXEL

Your painting is composed of thousands of dots, one next to the other. These dots are called picture elements, or 'pixels'.

A painting that is 640 dots wide and 480 tall has 307,200 pixels. Paint, like most graphics programs, works with pixel co-ordinates to indicate position. For example, the third pixel in from the left on the fourth line of pixels has the coordinates 3,4.

Often, when drawing lines, adding text or moving parts of the picture around, you need to position items precisely, so make a mental note of the coordinates each time.

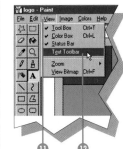

If you can't see the Fonts toolbar (shown above), you need to use Paint's menus to make it appear.

11 Click on the word View in the Menu bar.

12 Click Text Toolbar from the drop-down list.

13 Type a name.

14 Click on the typeface list and choose a prominent font.

15 Click on the size list to change the size.

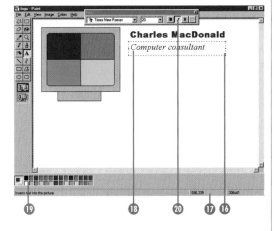

16 Draw another text box.

17 Keep an eye on the first number in the coordinates panel to make sure it's exactly the same as in step 10.

18 Type the job title.

19 Choose a color from the color palette.

20 Use the Italics button to change the job title text.

21 Add text for the other information – address, telephone number, etc. – in the same way, making sure to use the same X coordinate each time.

If you make a mistake, don't worry – you can always paint a white rectangle to cover up any errors, and try again (see page 63 for details of how to use the Rectangle drawing tool).

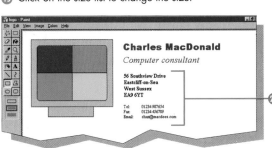

Drawing freehand

Paint's freehand drawing power and its wide range of color effects can be used to create simple pictures very quickly. This project shows how to design a T-shirt and a pair of shorts.

We've already seen that with Microsoft Paint it's easy to draw shapes and fill them in with any color. The next trick to learn is freehand drawing – using the mouse to draw the outline of your shapes instead of using ready-made circles and rectangles.

Freehand drawing on your computer is one of those easy to learn, but hard to master skills. At its simplest, you can start by doodling: draw some simple lines and curves and try to get the hang of moving the mouse while looking at the screen.

● **Getting started**
You can draw freehand using the Pencil tool or the Brush tool. In this exercise, we'll use the Brush (right) and start with a simple exercise to show basic drawing principles. With practice, a clean mouse (see page 91) and patience, you'll soon get the hang of it.

You'll find that Paint's brushes are a lot more versatile than the real thing! You can change their shape and size instantly, and there's no messy clean-up to worry about.

USING THE ERASER TOOL

Drawing freehand can be quite tricky at first – you'll often find that you're not as adept with your mouse as you are with a real paintbrush.

As usual, practice makes perfect, but in the meantime, you'll probably need to use the Eraser tool. This helps you correct any mistakes by rubbing out areas in your painting – you control how much or how little. In the drawing of a T-shirt (far right), the line we've drawn for the shoulder is too long. Here's how to erase it:

1. Move the pointer onto the toolbox and click on the Eraser (right), second from the top on the left-hand side.

2. A box displaying different eraser sizes appears below the toolbox. Click on the second one down so that it is highlighted, and move your mouse over

the drawing. The pointer becomes a small square to show that the Eraser is active.

3. Position the square over the part of the image that you want to erase. Hold down the left or right mouse button and drag the mouse carefully to erase – as you would using a rubber eraser on a pencil drawing.

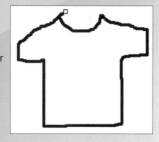

4. You can use the color palette to select the color for the erased area. For example, for a white background, you would click the right mouse button on white in the palette.

Drawing a team T-shirt

Here's how to use your computer to draw and color simple freehand shapes. We've used a sports T-shirt example to show you how to achieve fast results with the paintbrush.

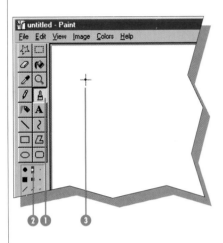

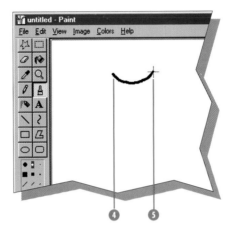

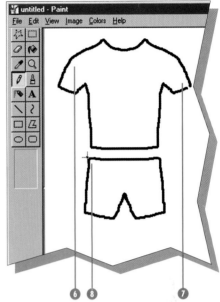

❶ Click on the Brush icon in the toolbox. A panel appears below with brush options.
❷ Click on the middle dot in the top row of brush shapes which appear below the toolbox. This sets the width and shape of the brush.
❸ Move the mouse pointer to where you want to begin drawing the T-shirt – near the top of the screen so that you leave enough space for a pair of shorts below.

❹ Hold down the left mouse button and, using smooth and easy movements, practice drawing the scoop neck of a T-shirt.
❺ When you have completed the outline, release the mouse button. Don't worry about getting things perfect right now – you can undo your last three changes, one at a time, by pressing the [Ctrl] and [Z] keys together.

❻ Once you are comfortable using the mouse to draw, add the sleeves and the outline of the body in the same way.
❼ If there are any gaps in your drawing, it's a simple matter to correct them; just go back and use the brush to join up the gap.
❽ Now move the pointer below the T-shirt. Hold down the left button and, in the same way you did with the T-shirt, draw some shorts.

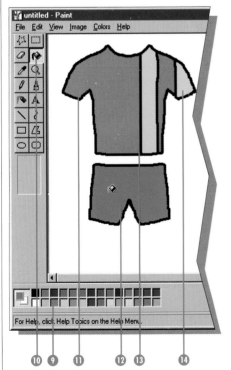

❾ Click on a color from the palette at the bottom of the screen. Let's try the bright red on the bottom row. (You will see red in the front square to the left of the palette to indicate that it is the active color.)
❿ Go back to the toolbox and click on the Fill tool (the tipping paint can).
⓫ Move the paint can cursor inside the outline of the T-shirt and press once on the left mouse button. The T-shirt fills with your chosen color.
⓬ Repeat steps 9 to 11 for the shorts, using the dark blue from the bottom row of the palette.
⓭ Of course, you can go back to the freehand paintbrush at any time you like – even after you've filled in the T-shirt. Here we've added some vertical stripes with the paintbrush.
⓮ Then we filled alternate stripes with yellow to create a sports-team look.

You can experiment with the colors of the shorts and the T-shirt as often as you wish, simply repeating steps 9 to 13 and picking up a different color from the palette.

Wallpaper your Windows Desktop

If you're bored with your standard Windows Desktop, why not create your own? With Paint, you can draw a new wallpaper pattern and cover your Desktop with it. Here's how.

Whenever your PC is switched on, Windows checks to see if you want a background 'wallpaper' design on your Desktop. Even if you haven't chosen one yourself, you might find that your PC manufacturer installed one for you.

Sometimes, new computers are set to show the famous Windows blue sky and clouds on the Desktop. Often, there is no wallpaper at all, just a solid background color. Whatever you see on your Desktop, you're not stuck with it forever – personalizing your computer by creating your own wallpaper with Microsoft Paint is very simple.

Just like real wallpaper, the overall effect is created by repeating a pattern both horizontally and vertically. Making patterns in Paint is simple and there's no reason why you can't have different wallpaper every day. It's up to your imagination.

You don't have to be a great artist to liven up your workplace – even simple images look stunning when repeated all over your Desktop.

Redecorating your computer

Like the paper on your living-room wall, Desktop wallpaper can really change your PC's personality. Here's how four simple designs alter the look and feel of the same computer.

Businesslike blue

Classically carved stone

Black thatch

Red tiles

Wallpapering the Desktop

To make your own wallpaper, you first need to create your own design in Paint. After that, a simple Paint menu option will set Windows to show it on your Desktop.

1 Open the Paint program from the Windows Start menu. Before painting anything, click on the Image menu and click on the Attributes command.

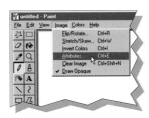

2 Type in a height of 100 pixels and a width of 100 pixels to create a small square. Click the OK button.

3 Now you can start to create your basic pattern. You can use any of Paint's tools; experiment to see what works best for your type of design.

We have chosen a starfish pattern. First we filled the whole image with black paint, then we roughly painted our starfish with yellow using the Airbrush tool (the fifth tool down on the left of the toolbar).

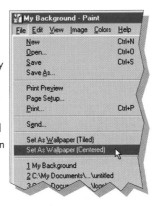

4 Now you have created your wallpaper pattern, you must save it. Select Save As from the File menu, and then save the file with a distinctive and obvious name, such as 'My Background'. Type the name you want to use in the File name: text box, and click the Save button.
Now your file is saved in case you want to alter it later.

5 Paint is well integrated with Windows – it will make all the changes necessary for your pattern to appear on the Windows Desktop with a single mouse click from you. All you need to do is click on the File menu and select the Set As Wallpaper (Centered) command.

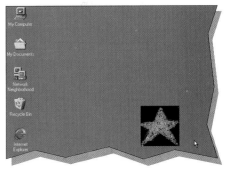

6 As soon as you select this menu command, Paint will send Windows a message to add your wallpaper to the Desktop. Click on the Paint window's Minimize button to see the effect. Your pattern appears right in the middle of the Desktop.

7 This centered picture is fine if you ever want to create a large painting to use as a single Desktop picture. What you really need for a simple small image such as this is to use it as a repeating pattern.

Paint also has this option covered. Click on the File menu, then choose the Set As Wallpaper (Tiled) option from the list of commands. Minimize the Paint window again to see the effect it has.

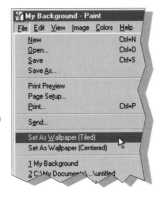

8 This time you'll see that your pattern starts in the top left corner and is repeated all the way across and down the screen. As you experiment, you'll see that some types of pattern work better than others.

Be careful about your color choices – just as when you decorate at home, lively colors can prove tiring after a while. At least redecorating your Windows Desktop only takes moments.

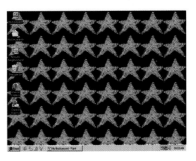

PC TIPS

Painting in two colors

When you're painting in Microsoft Paint, there's a quick way to paint in two colors without having to move to and from the color palette to keep switching colors. First, use the left mouse button to select one color from the palette, then use the right mouse button to choose the other – you'll see the two colors you choose displayed on the left of the color palette (left). Now, when you drag your mouse to paint your image, the left mouse button will paint in one color and the right mouse button will paint in the other.

Painting in detail

Sometimes when you want to draw very accurately, a magnifying glass and special pens or brushes are useful. Here's how to work in detail on your computer with Paint's versions of these tools.

If you've ever done any close-up and detailed drawing with normal pens and pencils, you'll know how helpful it is to have a ruler and a magnifying glass handy. It's the same when you use your computer to paint, except of course that you don't use the real-life tools. Instead, almost all graphics programs provide a way to zoom in on a painting, and show guidelines to make it easy to paint accurately.

With these tools, you can zoom in until you can see the individual pixels that make up your picture. You can then change them one by one. Combine this with guidelines available on your computer, and you have very precise control over the alignment of all the elements in your painting.

● Paint's tools
Paint's versions of these tools are the Magnifier, which lets you zoom in to show pixels up to eight times larger than normal, and a grid of pixels that you can switch on and off as required. Once zoomed in, you can edit individual pixels – this means that you can change the color of each pixel in your painting. Of course, it would be slow to paint a whole picture like this, but it's ideal for touching up small details in an image.

● Pick out the pixels
The Magnifier tool is accessible from the toolbar on the left of the Paint window. If you want to control the zoom level

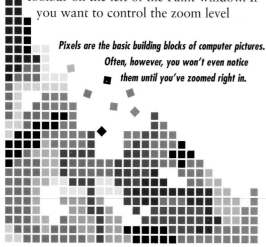

Pixels are the basic building blocks of computer pictures. Often, however, you won't even notice them until you've zoomed right in.

Paint is designed to allow you to work in extreme close-up for fine detail work. Use the Zoom and Magnifier tools to change your painting pixel by pixel.

precisely, you can select Zoom from the View menu and choose the Custom option that allows you to specify the percentage level of magnification you want.

When you have zoomed in close, you can also turn on Paint's pixel grid. This helps you get perfect alignment in your pictures. Select Zoom from the View menu, and choose the Show Grid option.

There's also a Show Thumbnail option, which displays a small picture of your whole painting to remind you what effect the changes you make will have when you see the painting back at its normal size.

● Going in close
If Paint didn't provide these tools it would be frustrating, if not impossible, to do any close-up work. What's more, being able to zoom in is useful for more than just accurate alignment. Sometimes, when you use the Fill tool to paint big areas, the color leaks out and affects other parts of your image. Zooming in allows you to find and plug the individual pixels to close the hole.

WHAT IT MEANS

GRID

Most graphics programs use the concept of a grid to help you align parts of your painting. In Paint, the grid is a set of horizontal and vertical lines you can see when you are zoomed in – it looks like graph paper, and the pixels you paint fill the individual squares.

Zooming in on a picture to edit fine detail

You can achieve some truly remarkable results when you zoom in to change fine detail in a picture. By repainting individual pixels on your Desktop icons, you can even give them a gold-plated effect!

1 Open Paint and position it so that you can see the My Computer icon to the left, as shown here. Press the [PrintScreen] key (it's on the top row of your keyboard toward the right). This takes a snapshot of the whole screen, and copies it into the Clipboard (see pages 16–17).

2 Click on Paint's Edit menu and select Paste. You might see a dialog box (inset) asking you if you want to increase the size of the **bitmap** to take the image stored in the Clipboard. Click the Yes button.

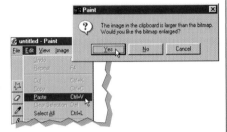

WHAT IT MEANS

BITMAP

A bitmap is a computer picture made up of row upon row of pixels. All Paint pictures are bitmaps. Other types, such as drawings and illustrations from programs like CorelDRAW, are made of individual objects you can move and edit such as lines, circles and shapes. Such pictures are called vector graphics.

3 You'll see the snapshot of your Windows screen appear in the Paint working area. We've used this 'screen-grabbing' technique to provide a ready-made image to use to demonstrate how to edit individual pixels.

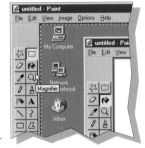

4 Click on View, then Zoom and Custom. A dialog box appears: click on the 800% option and then click on the OK button.

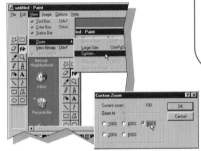

5 The image increases in size and now you can clearly see the individual pixels that make up the small My Computer icon. Click on the Fill tool and select the light yellow paint from the palette. Replace all the white pixels in the original My Computer icon with yellow paint by clicking on each pixel.

6 As you work, you'll find it's hard to imagine the effect on the normal-size image. You may be unsure about the choice of yellow paint. Click the View menu, Zoom and then select Show Thumbnail.

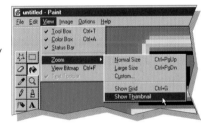

7 Select the olive green paint above the yellow, and replace all of the light gray pixels in the My Computer icon.

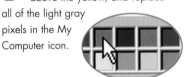

8 Now, as you replace the gray pixels one by one, the small thumbnail window shows how your pixel editing affects the real (i.e. normal-size) image.

9 Click on the brown paint from the far right of the palette and replace all of the dark gray pixels in the icon.

10 Notice that while the picture in the painting area still looks yellow and brown, the normal size version in the thumbnail looks a gorgeous gold color. This is a visual effect: the human eye doesn't see the individual yellow and brown pixels; it averages adjacent pixels and 'sees' different colors.

11 We've continued to color in the other icons from the Desktop, using the same color-replacing scheme detailed above. As you can see, the result is a gold-plated set of icons that seems impossible to create from just yellow and brown paint!

For now, save this painting using the normal File and Save As menu options. Call it 'gold icons.bmp'. Later in the course, we'll show you how to replace your standard Desktop icons with these icons (or any other images you want).

Duplicating parts of your pictures

Real painters who want to duplicate part of a picture have to do it the hard way – by hand. For computer users, there's no such problem; by using Paint's two powerful selection tools, you can duplicate an item in seconds.

If you've been following the exercises in Word, you have seen how you can use the mouse to select words in a document and then how to copy and paste them as many times as you like. You can do the same with a graphics program such as Microsoft Paint. In Paint, you can select any part of your picture and then delete it, copy it and paste it anywhere you like – you can even paste it into another picture.

Being able to copy parts of your painting and then paste them elsewhere can be a real time-saver. Imagine you want to create a picture of a tree with lots of leaves on it. It might take ages to paint all the individual leaves but, if you paint one good one, you can copy and paste it many times all over the tree to create the effect you want.

● Two selection tools
Paint provides two tools to help you select parts of your painting. There's a rectangular one that lets you select simple square or rectangular parts, and there's a free-form tool, with which you can select any shape from your painting.

To use the rectangular selection tool, go to the toolbar at the left of the Paint window and click on the

Paint is a great tool with which to be creative with your PC. Simple designs can become works of art.

top-right button (that's the one with a dotted rectangle on it). Return to the painting area and drag with your mouse to select the part of the painting you're interested in.

The advantage of the rectangular Select tool is that it's very quick and easy to use. The downside is that you can only select rectangular areas. However, this is ideal if you want to copy or delete whole items that aren't joined to another part of your picture.

● Free form
To use the Free-Form Select tool, click on the button at the top left of the toolbar – it has a dotted star on it. To use this in the painting area, hold down the left mouse button and drag the tool around the edges of the object you're copying. We show you how to do this in detail on the opposite page.

You can copy any part of a picture by highlighting it and using the Copy and Paste options on the Edit menu.

S H O R T C U T S

When you're doing lots of copy and paste actions, remember that keyboard shortcuts can help you work more quickly. When you've selected an area, press [Ctrl]+[C] to copy it, then [Ctrl]+[V] to paste it.

How to make multiple copies

Use Paint's selection tools to cut out repetitive painting and turn one of your paintings into a greeting card. Here we show you how copy and paste works in Paint.

Microsoft®Paint

DRAWING A STAR

To draw a star in Paint, use the Polygon tool. This lets you draw straight edges that Paint will form into a solid shape. Select the tool and move the mouse pointer to the painting area. Click and hold down the left mouse button as you drag to draw the first edge. Release the button, move the pointer to the position you want the next corner to be in and click once: Paint will draw the second edge. Repeat this process for each edge until you are back at the start of your first line.

1 Here's our star, which we are going to copy and paste (see Drawing A Star, left). It is an irregular shape so we'll use the Free-Form Select tool. Choose this by clicking on the top left button on the toolbar.

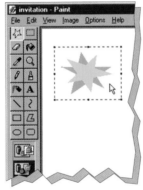

3 Work your way around the star and try to finish close to your starting point before you release the mouse button. If you don't start and finish at exactly the same point, Paint will wait for you to finish, then tidy things up. Finally, a dotted rectangle will appear around the selected area.

2 Now go across to the painting area, move the mouse close to the star, click and hold down the left button and start to trace carefully around the outside of the star. As you move the mouse, a black line will appear to show the perimeter of the area.

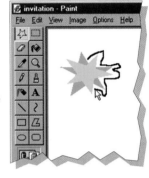

4 Click on the top option of the two color pictures shown in the lower section of the toolbar, this is called the Opaque option. Then choose Copy from the Edit menu. This makes a copy of this part of your picture in the Windows Clipboard.

5 Before you paste the star, draw a black rectangle to the right of your painting. Now paste a copy of the star by choosing Paste from the Edit menu. Drag and drop this copy of the star over the black area. You'll see that the star's white rectangle outline is also pasted. This is because the Opaque option was selected when we pasted the star from the Clipboard.

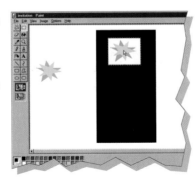

6 Often, it's useful to paste without the surrounding rectangle. To do this, click over the bottom of the two options shown under the toolbar (this is called the Transparent option, below left). Paste and drag the star over the black area. Because the background color is white (shown right, in the two color squares at the left of the color palette), Paint treats the white area in the pasted copy as transparent.

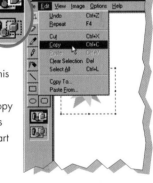

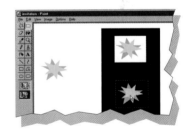

7 Save time by pasting as many stars as you like onto your invitation. Once you've duplicated an item, you can use Paint's other tools on it. We've used the Flip/Rotate option (left) from the Image menu to rotate each star. We've also changed the colors of the stars using the Fill tool (see pages 62–63). On the right is the finished card.

PLEASE COME TO MY BIRTHDAY PARTY

Your toolbox guide

The key to getting the best from Microsoft Paint is finding out which tools are at your disposal and what you can do with them. Let's dip into the Paint toolbox and review all the 16 available tools to see which are best suited to each job.

If you want to get the most out of Microsoft Paint, it's vital to get comfortable with its toolbox. By now, you know what some of the 16 buttons on the toolbox are for and how to use them. Let's take this opportunity to revise what we've already learned and also to fill in the gaps about the other buttons in the toolbox.

On pages 72–73, we saw how the top two buttons select areas of a drawing so that they can be cut from it and pasted somewhere else. The top-left button is the Free-Form Select tool and it allows you to draw freehand around an area to select it. This takes a steady hand to master, but there's always the quicker and easier (if less precise) normal Select tool which you can access from the top-right button on the toolbox. This allows you to select rectangular areas of your drawing.

In the second row
The two buttons on the second row of the toolbox are the Eraser tool and the Fill tool. You can use the Eraser to rub out parts of your drawing and you can choose different sizes for the tool to suit the amount of rubbing out you want to do.

The Fill tool allows you to flood an enclosed area with the currently selected painting color.

The third row of buttons consists of the Pick tool and the Magnifier tool. The first one allows you to pick up the color of any part of your drawing and make it the currently selected color.

The Magnifier lets you zoom in on any part of your drawing

to see fine details and choose different levels of magnification to suit your needs.

Drawing freehand lines
The Pencil and Brush tools are on the fourth row. These tools provide different styles for drawing freehand lines. A Pencil line is always only one pixel wide, but you can choose a variety of widths and shapes with the Brush.

The Airbrush tool on the fifth row gives you another way of freehand painting on your drawing and offers three different sizes of airbrush.

Next to it is the Text tool, which lets you include text in a variety of sizes, fonts and weights.

Shapes and lines
The sixth row holds the related Line and Curve tools. Line is used to draw straight lines while Curve lets you include smooth curves as part of your drawing.

The last two rows provide you with tools to draw a variety of shapes. The buttons on the seventh row let you draw rectangles and other polygons. The eighth row has tools to draw ellipses and rectangles with rounded corners.

Most of the tools found in a conventional artist's bag are also to be found in the Paint toolbox.

SHORT CUTS

When working close-up on a Paint drawing you often want to see as much of the drawing as possible, so hide the Paint toolbox from view by pressing the [Ctrl] and [T] keys. When you want to see the toolbox again, just press the same two keys.

Get to know your Paint tools

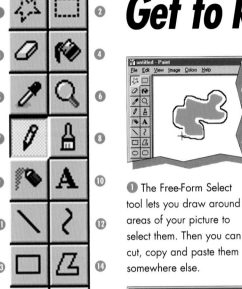

1 The Free-Form Select tool lets you draw around areas of your picture to select them. Then you can cut, copy and paste them somewhere else.

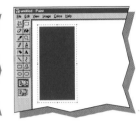

2 The normal Select tool lets you select rectangular areas of your drawing. Then you can cut the areas or copy and paste them to another position.

3 The Eraser tool lets you rub out parts of a drawing. You can choose the size of this tool by clicking on one of the shapes shown below the toolbox.

4 The Fill tool allows you to fill an area of one color (or no color at all) with another color.

5 The Pick tool lets you select a color from within your drawing to be the current drawing color. This is helpful for getting exact color matches.

6 The Magnifier tool lets you zoom in on a selected area of your drawing. You can choose the level of magnification from the options below the toolbox.

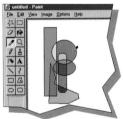

7 The Pencil tool allows you to draw freehand lines exactly one pixel wide. You can choose the color you want to draw in from the Paint palette.

8 The Brush tool lets you draw freehand lines with a brush effect. You can choose the style and size of brush from the options shown below the toolbox.

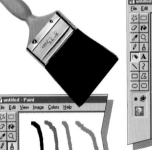

9 The Airbrush tool allows you to paint areas with an airbrush effect. You can choose the size of this tool from the three offered below the toolbox.

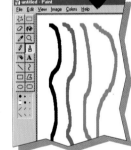

10 The Text tool lets you type text into your drawing. You can choose the size, weight and font of the words you type.

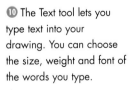

11 The Line tool allows you to draw straight lines in the currently selected drawing color. You can choose the width of line you want from the ones shown below the toolbox.

12 The Curve tool allows you to draw curves in the currently selected drawing color.

13 The Rectangle tool lets you draw rectangles and squares. You can choose whether the shape is filled or just an outline from the options available below the toolbox. The Rounded Rectangle **16** is used in the same way if you want to have rounded corners on the shapes.

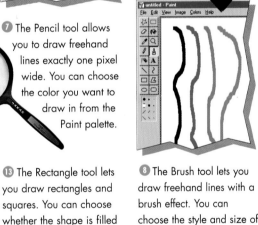

14 The Polygon tool lets you draw freehand polygons like this complex shape. You can choose if the polygon is filled in or is just an outline by selecting one of the options below the toolbox.

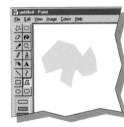

15 The Ellipse tool lets you draw ellipses and circles. You can choose whether it is filled with color or is just an outline.

Special effects in Paint

Paint has more to offer than the functions available via the toolbox. Here's how to exploit a group of easy-to-use special effects hidden away in one of Paint's menus.

Practice will help you become familiar with the tools offered in Paint and, as you get used to using this software, you'll discover that it has hidden depths. You'll develop your own quick ways to achieve the results you want.

However, there's one really useful set of functions you won't find if you only ever use the toolbox. Hidden away in the Image menu are several effects that you can apply to achieve even more creative drawings. Using these different text effects and illustrations will inject a little bit more pizzazz into your letters and greeting cards.

By default, Paint applies these special effects to the whole drawing when you use them. However, you can use the Select and Free-Form Select tools to specify particular areas of your drawing where you want the special effects to be applied. For example, you can use these effects to modify text or even just a single letter in a

sentence, as well as to alter shapes or objects in your drawing.

● **Types of special effects**
There are two main types of special effects you can achieve. First, the Flip/Rotate option in the Image menu gives you the power to rotate your drawing (or a selected part of it) through 90, 180 or 270 degrees, or to flip it horizontally or vertically. Second, you can stretch or skew your drawing (or a selected part of it) by using the Stretch/Skew option in the Image menu.

A special dialog box will appear if you choose Flip/Rotate from the Image menu. Here you can simply click on the appropriate button to choose whether you want to flip your drawing horizontally, flip it vertically or rotate it. If you choose the rotation option, then you have the further choice of angle from 90, 180 or 270 degrees. Once you've chosen the effect you want, click the OK button and wait to see the results.

● **Stretch and Skew**
Similarly, another special dialog box will appear if you choose the Stretch/Skew option. This time it offers you the choice of four effects: horizontal stretch, vertical stretch, horizontal skew or vertical skew. Simply click on the appropriate button for the effect you want. If you choose a stretch, you can type in the percentage by which you want to stretch your drawing; if you choose a skew, you can type in the angle at which you want your drawing skewed.

Create various eye-catching designs for your cards and letters by using Paint's Stretch and Skew options.

Special effects with the Image menu

The tools in Paint's Image menu allow you to create some interesting effects with text and basic graphics – perfect for adding a little sparkle to your text documents, greetings cards and business cards.

1 Let's start by typing in some sample red text. With the left mouse button, select red as the foreground color from the palette at the bottom left of the screen. Click on the Text tool in the toolbox and draw a text box. Type in some words.

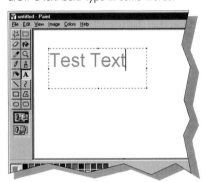

2 Let's see what happens when we stretch the words. Select Stretch/Skew from the Image menu. In the dialog box that appears, type '400' into the vertical percentage box and click on the OK button. After a short wait, you'll see the finished effect (see below, inset).

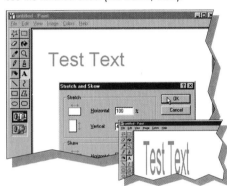

3 To add a skew effect to the text, select the text with the Select tool and then Stretch/Skew from the image menu. Type '30' into the Horizontal degrees box in the Skew section and click OK. The result will appear (below, inset).

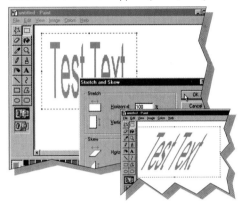

4 You can also type in negative numbers for the skew effect to achieve a 'reverse' italic image. Use the Text tool to create some new plain text and type '-30' into the Horizontal degrees box in the Skew section.

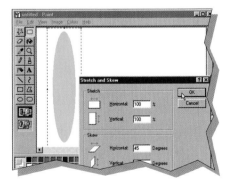

5 When you press the OK button, the Paint program slants the text from the upper left to lower right. You can apply the same principle to skewing parts of your picture vertically and skew the elements either to the left or to the right. Experiment to see the effects you can get.

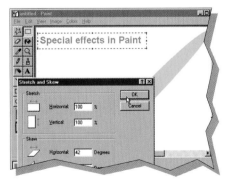

6 Now let's combine some effects on shapes and text. Set yellow as the foreground color and use the Ellipse tool to draw an outline shape. Then use the Fill tool to fill it with yellow. Next, select the shape with the Select tool and use Stretch/Skew from the Image menu. Apply a 45-degree horizontal skew.

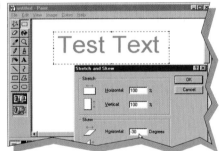

7 Make red the foreground color, type in some words and then use the Select tool to select a rectangular area around them. Next, choose Stretch/Skew from the Image menu and this time apply a vertical skew to the selected area – we've used one of 42 degrees.

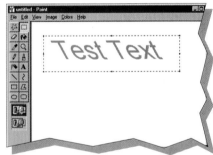

8 Notice that a rectangular area around the skewed text is still selected, but its dimensions have changed. The final step is to move this area over the yellow ellipse, so click somewhere inside the rectangle, hold down the left mouse button and drag and drop the text to position it accurately.

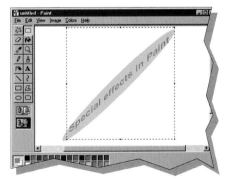

Designing a Christmas card

Creating images can be quick and easy on your PC. With the help of Microsoft Paint and a little practice, you can create stylish designs for anything, from labels to greeting cards.

MERRY CHRISTMAS

I n the step-by-step exercises on pages 62–77, you have learned how to use some of the most important Paint commands and tricks, as well as the tools in the toolbox. Now, by combining all that you have learned, it's possible to produce professional looking pictures. To start, we will show you how to produce an attractive Christmas card cover.

A little planning before you begin will make your task easier. First, form in your mind a clear picture of what you want to draw and then think about how you are going to achieve it. There isn't a specific tool for every job, so you must use lateral thinking to achieve the best results. If you're going to include text, remember to leave space for it on your design. Also, consider the colors you are

going to use. Try to choose colors that will stand out against the background you are using. Some shapes might need to be outlines, so you can use Paint's built-in tools to help you with a lot of the work. Some of the figures might turn out to be quite easy to draw using the Ellipse or Rectangle tool.

● **Drawing something different**
At this point, you might even consider changing parts of your picture if you see an easy way to draw something different. Although you will see examples in the step-by-step guide opposite, don't be afraid to add your own ideas and techniques as you go along.

Making your card

Paint's variety of tools can be used to create all sorts of images. Here we show you how to achieve great results.

1 We need a landscape. It's Christmas, so that means a white ground and blue sky. Choose blue from the color palette by left-clicking on it. Click the Line tool and draw a line horizontally across the screen. To make sure the line goes right across the page, you will probably have to move the scroll bar to the right. Select the Fill tool (inset) and color in the top half of the picture.

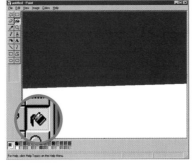

2 Next, use the Ellipse tool (inset) to draw a snowman's head and body. First, select the color black from the palette: as you are drawing the snowman on top of a partially white background, you must make sure he stands out. Next, select the Ellipse tool. Place the cursor where you want his body to start, then drag it across until the circle is big enough. It may take a couple of attempts to get it right, so undo your last action to revert to the previous version if you make a mistake. Use the same method to draw the head on top.

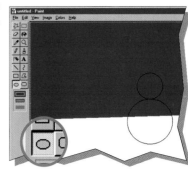

3 Now color in the snowman. Select white as the foreground color and fill in the circles. Add some eyes and a mouth by selecting black again and choosing the Brush tool (left inset). Change the brush type to produce a dot wherever you click on the screen (right inset).

4 The next thing to draw is a Christmas tree, using the Polygon tool (inset left). First, select a shade of green as the foreground color. Next, select the Polygon tool and click the bottom fill option. Decide where the top of your tree is going to be and click and drag the outline of the tree. When you have finished, double-click and your tree will be filled in and drawn.

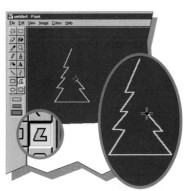

5 To draw snowflakes, use the Text tool and asterisks. Click the cursor where you want a snowflake and the Text toolbar will appear. Select the Times New Roman font, a large font size, such as 26, and type a single asterisk by pressing [Shift] and [8]. It's easiest to create more asterisks by drawing a box around the first asterisk using the Select tool and then using the Copy and Paste commands from the Edit menu to duplicate them. You can also draw snowflakes using the Wingdings font.

6 Add a brown rectangle as a tree trunk, then write a greeting using the Text tool (see pages 64–65). Use a solid color and large text so that it stands out against the snow.

(see pages 64–65)

WHAT IT MEANS

WINGDINGS

The Wingdings font can create better 'snowflakes' than those drawn in step 5. Select Wingdings by clicking on the first box on the Text toolbar and scrolling down the list. Press the [T] key and a snowflake appears.

7 The final touch is to add some clouds. For this, the Airbrush tool is ideal. Select the Airbrush tool and choose the largest spray size. Make sure that the foreground color is white. Spray a shape in the sky to look like a wintry cloud.

8 You can leave the card like this, or spend a little more time adding some extra details, such as a star for the tree and a scarf and hat for the snowman (made with the Polygon tool) and some Christmas balls (made with the Ellipse tool). Have fun and don't be afraid to experiment!

Choosing new colors

At first sight it may appear that Microsoft Paint allows you to choose only a few colors with which to draw pictures. However, you can add many more shades by creating your own customized colors.

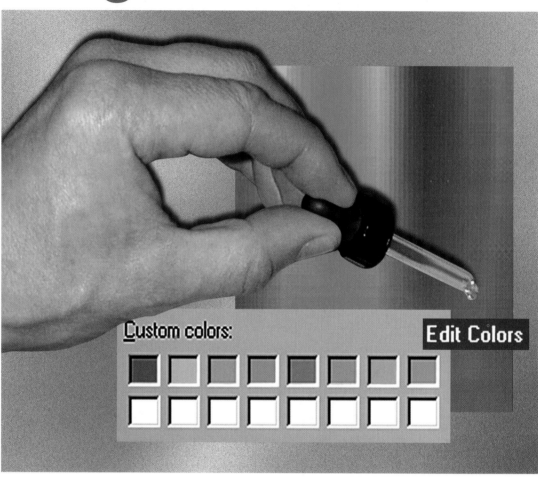

Custom colors: Edit Colors

While working with Paint, you might find that you feel a little restricted by the choice of colors available, because there are only 28 colors in the color palette shown at the bottom of the screen.

For simple pictures, these colors are adequate to get your ideas across. They cover all the main options – reds, yellows, blues and so on. They are very useful for bold graphics and cartoon-style images with lots of contrast. However, as there are few shades of the same color, subtle shading effects are not possible.

● Palette picker

Fortunately, Paint provides you with a way to choose any color you like. Paint's color picker dialog box lets you change an existing palette color to any other color you wish. While there are various ways to specify new colors, the best method for those with only a little experience of graphics packages is to choose

new colors by pointing and clicking on the screen. The color picker dialog box provides a large multicolored square. You just click on the square at a color you want and then click on a button to add it to your own custom color palette. Once you have created your new color palette, you can use it in any of your other paintings.

● Dotty display

When you choose and customize colors, you might find that some of them appear to be 'dotted'. This is called 'dithering' and occurs when Windows cannot show the true color you have chosen. The way to avoid dithered colors is to run your computer screen in 'true color.' This is a mode that shows all colors without any dithering at all. You can choose this mode from the Display Properties window, which is accessed by right-clicking on the Desktop and choosing Properties from the menu that appears.

WHAT IT MEANS

DITHERING
By using two color combinations, Windows can simulate a third, intermediate color. This process, called dithering, is often required when you are using the computer while it is running in 256-color mode.

When working on graphics, dithering is distracting. The solution is to change to true color mode (we will cover this in detail later in the course).

Custom colors

Pick and choose, from reds to blues and any color in between, to make your own shades and tones.

CREATING YOUR own customized colors can be extremely handy when you need to work with several different shades of one color. For example, it would be particularly useful if you wanted to draw a realistic sky, graduating from white through to pale blue and then a darker blue, or perhaps a grass background with varying shades of green. In the example shown below, we'll be choosing colors with which to draw a simple sea and sky. They will change from a medium blue at the bottom to a dark blue at the top.

Microsoft® Paint

1 Open Paint and double-click anywhere on the color palette to make the Edit Colors window appear.

2 Click on the Define Custom Colors button. You'll now see a window with a rainbow of colors displayed (right). From here, you can pick a specific color from anywhere in the spectrum. (The numbers below the main window relate to the color currently selected.)

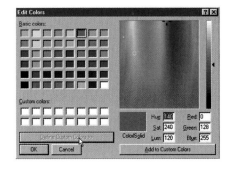

PC TIPS

If you want to use lots of colors in Paint, you will need to instruct Windows to display the highest number of colors possible. In 256-color mode, you can see a lot of dithering of colors, while in 24-bit true color mode all the colors are displayed without any dithering at all. (Note that on some computers 24-bit color is called 32-bit color.)

The colors in the box above are dithered in 256 colors; the same colours in 24-bit true color mode shown in the box below look fine.

3 The first color we want is a medium blue. Move the cursor into the blue area of the window. Then move it to the top middle of the blue so that you select a bright blue color. The color you choose will be shown in the Color/Solid box. A range of colors, both lighter and darker, will also be shown in the band to the right of the color window, arranged around the shade you have selected.

4 Click on the Add to Custom Colors button. This will move the selected color into the Custom colors box.

5 It is worth setting all the shades of one particular color at a time. By doing this, you will be able to compare shades as you go along. Click on an empty box in the Custom colors grid where the new color can go.

6 Now click in the same area of blue, but this time select a visibly darker shade. This is done by clicking on the tall, thin shaded band to the right of the large color square. When you have found the shade that you want, press Add to Custom Colors.

7 Repeat this process and continue to select further shades of your chosen color until you have at least six progressively darker shades stored in the Custom colors grid.

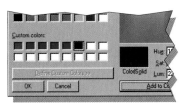

8 You can now add your new shades of blue to a drawing that requires them. Even a simple picture will often benefit from using a range of subtle custom shades that would not be possible using Paint's standard palette.

Now you've mastered the basics of Microsoft Paint, there are all sorts of practical uses for your new skills. For instance, here's how you can quickly create a simple and effective map showing directions to a garage sale.

Painting a map

You should by now be familiar with how to use all the tools on Microsoft Paint's toolbar (see pages 74–75), as well as the more advanced features hidden away in its menus (see pages 76–77). The only limit on how creative you can be is your own imagination – all it takes is a little patience and practice.

For example, let's imagine you've volunteered to do the publicity leaflets for a neighbor's garage sale. The text part of the leaflet is straightforward and can easily be created in a Microsoft Word document. However, you now need to add some directions about how to get to the garage sale. The best way is to provide a map, so let's make an attempt at this by using Paint. Remember, we'll be able to take the finished Paint map and insert it into our Word document (see PC Tips, right).

● Combination of Paint skills
Drawing a map requires a combination of Paint tools and skills (see opposite, Creating a simple map). If you're not quite sure where to start, it might be a good idea to make a rough pencil and paper sketch to work from.

The first thing to do in Paint is to use the Pencil tool to sketch in the roads freehand –

it doesn't matter if your mouse control is a bit shaky at first, you can always start again from the beginning. A good tip is to save your map each time you complete a correct stage of drawing it. Then, if you make a mistake, you can just close your document without saving it and reopen the last version you did save.

Once the roads are finished, it's easy to include buildings by using the Rectangle tool. Other elements (such as the duck pond in our example) can be added by using the Rectangle, Ellipse, Rounded Rectangle and Polygon tools. A neat way to include features such as churches or telephone boxes is to use the Text tool to add symbols from unusual Windows fonts, such as Wingdings (see page 79). The Fill and Airbrush tools are really handy for including countryside features, for example, trees, bushes and fields.

The last stage is to use the Text tool to label all the important landmarks on the map. Don't be restricted to adding horizontal text, as there's a clever way of including vertical text: use the Flip/Rotate option in the Image menu to rotate your map. Then you can add a text label and rotate the map back to its original position.

PC TIPS

You can include Paint drawings in Microsoft Word documents (see pages 44–47). Use the Select tool in Paint to choose part of your drawing, then select Copy from the Edit menu.

Switch to Word and choose Page Layout from the View menu. Paste from the Edit menu to insert the selected part of the drawing.

Creating a simple map

You can use all your accumulated knowledge of Paint to create a variety of useful graphics. Here's how to draw a map showing the directions to a local garage sale.

1 The first thing to do is sketch in the roads. Click on the Pencil tool in the toolbar, choose black from the palette and use the drag and drop technique to draw in the roads. We can use the Rectangle tool to add some buildings to our map. Click on the Rectangle tool button in the toolbar, choose the middle option from below the toolbar and select black as the foreground color and brown as the background color. Now just use your mouse to draw the required building shapes.

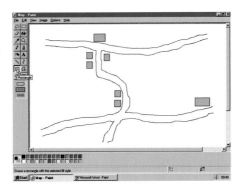

2 The next step is to add the duck pond. Keep black as the foreground color and choose blue as the new background color from the palette. Then click on the Ellipse button in the toolbar and use your mouse to add the pond.

3 Now we want to fill in a green area to denote the school playing field. We do this by first using the Line tool to draw a line between the loop in the road. Then we select the Fill tool and choose green as the foreground color, clicking on the area we want to fill.

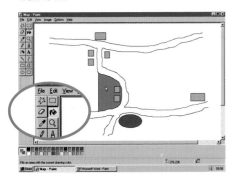

4 Next let's mark the position of the church with a cross. Select the Text tool and click where you want the church to be. If the Text toolbar doesn't appear, go to the View menu and select Text Toolbar. Then set 36pt Wingdings (see page 79) as the font and type a capital V to get a cross character.

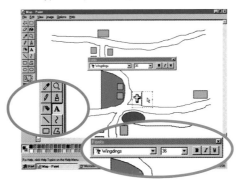

5 Don't forget the bushes beside the duck pond! Select green as the foreground color from the palette and click over the Airbrush button in the toolbar. Pick the largest spray area from the options and paint in the bushes by holding down the button and moving the mouse around.

6 Now we're ready to start labeling the map's key features. Choose black as the foreground color in the palette, click over the Text button in the toolbar and click where you want your first label to go. Choose a legible font, such as 12pt Times New Roman.

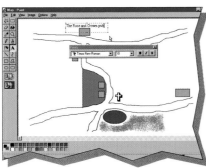

7 We have to label the playing fields vertically, so choose Flip/Rotate from the Image menu and rotate your map 90 degrees. Pick white as the foreground color and use the Text tool to add the label.

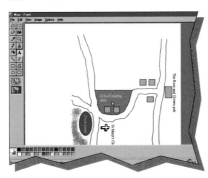

8 The final touch is to put the map back around the right way. Select Flip/Rotate again from the Image menu and this time rotate your map 270 degrees.

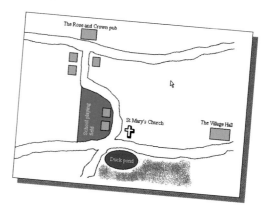

Know Paint's limits

Microsoft Paint offers a quick and easy way of creating simple graphics, such as party invitations, maps and logos. But this program does have its limitations.

P aint is a pixel-based painting program. This means that whenever you use its tools to create a picture, you are actually painting areas composed of individual dots (or pixels) in a new color. So, for example, if you use Paint's Pencil tool to draw a straight black line, you are really just changing the color of the pixels that make up the line to black.

This method of creating graphics by editing pixels is called bitmap painting and Paint is one of the best-known examples of a bitmap painting program. However, while programs like Paint are simple to use, they have limitations when it comes to creating more complicated graphics.

The first limitation of Paint is that once you've drawn something, the only way to modify it later is to change its pixels by drawing over them with something new.

For example, if you draw a filled red rectangle and want to come back later and change it to an unfilled rectangle with a blue outline, the only way to do it is by painting over the original drawing. It's just as awkward to change other aspects of the rectangle, such as its height and width.

● **No object**

These difficulties occur because any object you draw in Paint isn't stored as an object – it's simply an area of colored pixels. This limitation is more serious than it first appears. Here are some examples of the things you can't do because of it: you can't go back and change the typeface or size of any text in your picture; you can't go back and change the width of a line; and you can't go back and change a filled circle to an outline one.

We've also seen that you can move items around a Paint drawing using the various selection tools. The problem is that these tools select only an area of painted pixels rather than the objects themselves. This becomes a serious problem when you have items that overlap in a drawing. For example, if you have a square that overlaps a circle, you can't select the square and move it to reveal the circle behind. Another limitation of bitmap drawings becomes apparent when you try to enlarge them. What may look like a smooth line on your original drawing will turn into an ugly line full of jaggies when you try to make it bigger.

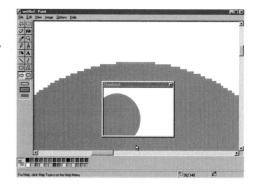

The more you enlarge a bitmap image, the more jagged the edges become. This is one of the main limitations of a pixel-based painting program such as Microsoft Paint.

Bitmaps versus vectors

For pictures unsuitable for bitmap painting programs, another type of graphics software is available. These programs are called drawing – or vector graphics – programs.

PAINT ALLOWS YOU to save your pictures in bitmap form only. There are, however, more sophisticated graphics programs – known as vector graphics programs – that overcome the main limitations of bitmaps (see below). For example, you can change any aspect of drawn objects, such as their width, outline and color, at any time because they are stored in the image as individual objects. In addition, these objects suffer no loss of quality or smoothness if you want to enlarge them. However, the extra sophistication of vector graphics programs means that they are harder to use. A bitmap painting package is the ideal choice for simple graphics, but for anything more ambitious, a drawing program is worth the effort.

In the next volume of *PCs made easy* we begin a step-by-step course for a vector graphics program – CorelDRAW.

Microsoft®Paint

1 Here is a Paint picture with three overlapping items: a green circle, a blue rectangle and a thick red line. Like most bitmap painting programs, Paint makes it easy to draw these things on top of each other, but remember we are really painting pixels rather than drawing objects.

2 As we've seen before in our Paint exercises, we can use the Select tool to select a rectangular region that contains the circle, rectangle and line. Then we can use the mouse to drag and drop them (as if they were a single item) to a new position in our drawing.

3 But what happens if we want to move the blue rectangle to a new position? If we use the Select tool we can choose a region that matches the area occupied by the rectangle. Let's see what happens when we try to move it to a new position.

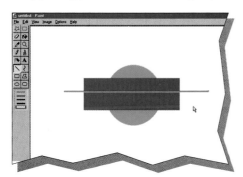

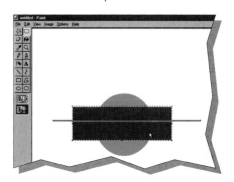

4 Now there's a problem: the Select tool only allows us to select an area of painted pixels, not a proper object. The trouble is that the selected area includes a portion of the red line and, because the green circle has been painted over, there's a hole where the rectangle used to be. The only way to get the drawing you want is to start another Paint drawing.

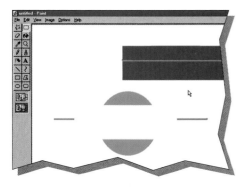

VECTOR DRAWING PROGRAMS

The key difference between a bitmap painting program and a vector drawing program is that the latter stores each item of a drawing as an individual object. You can select such an object simply by clicking on it and change its properties at any time. So, for instance, you can change the color, size and angle of rotation and many other aspects of an object. It's also easy to pick up an object and move it to another location in the drawing without harming any other objects that it may happen to overlap (shown right and above).

In fact, all the objects in a vector drawing program are stored as mathematical formulas by the program. The advantage of this is that if you change the size of the objects, they retain their smoothness. You can also alter a vector graphics object (by, for example, stretching or twisting it) and it will retain its smoothness.

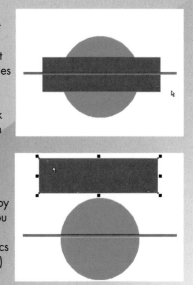

Hardware

The multimedia PC

You've bought your computer and set it up. But what are the parts that make up a PC?

Your home PC is a great example of evolution in action. From origins as a silent office computer, it has evolved into a magnificent all-singing, all-dancing multimedia system.

The main reason for its success is that no matter what you want to do with your PC, you can adapt it to take on completely new tasks. Your home PC shares perhaps 80 percent of its components with today's business PC, but with the addition of just a handful of extras, it can play music CDs, show movies and paint and print stunning color pictures.

● Bits and PCs

Each PC component is replaceable and that makes it easy to change one component for another. You can usually mix and match components from different PC makers, and that increases your options hugely. There are literally thousands of items to choose from.

For example, if you want your PC to go faster, you can often swap its processor for a faster one. Imagine being able to change a Ford's engine to one from a Ferrari!

Swapping components is only half the story; your PC can also grow to take on advances in technology that were hardly dreamed of when the

Keyboard

The keyboard allows you to type documents and input instructions that tell your PC what to do. It inherited its 'QWERTY' layout from the typewriter and has over 100 keys that give all the options you need to make the most of your PC's power and versatility.

Monitor

It might look like a TV screen, but in fact your monitor is much more powerful. Both can show full-color images, but your monitor can show pictures and text with much finer detail.

Speakers

Your PC's speakers are similar to the speakers you find in today's stereo radio cassette players. The main difference is that many PC speakers have their own built-in amplifier (powered by batteries or a transformer). A few also have a special bass speaker

Floppy disk drive

Floppy disks store only a small amount of data, and they are best used for transferring small files from one PC to another. The drive is part of the system unit, which is covered in more detail on page 90.

CD-ROM drive

CD-ROM disks can store large amounts of data. Use this drive to play music CDs, load software and games from CD-ROMs and even photographs from PhotoCDs.

Mouse

The mouse is essential for moving efficiently around the computer screen – as you move the mouse, the pointer moves on screen. A mouse usually has two buttons, although a few have three and some only one.

computer giant IBM first created the PC in the early 1980s.

Speakers, CD-ROM drives and even video cameras are already part of the multimedia experience. As well as making PCs more fun for home users, these expansion devices also make PCs capable of completely new jobs. Already it's possible to record movies onto the hard disk of your computer, edit them and add special effects, and then record them back onto video tape. The possibilities for the future are enormous.

● **Around the multimedia PC**

With all these replaceable and expandable components, your multimedia PC might seem like a confusing collection of boxes and wires. It can be hard work to figure out what does what and why.

In this tour around the multimedia PC, we'll show you how it all works together in harmony. We'll also lift the lid and take a look at what goes on inside the system unit itself. Knowing how the sum of the parts fits together is a great way to begin to get more from the whole.

Modem

A modem connects the computer to the outside world by telephone line. Most are fax/modems, which connect to the Internet and send and receive faxes directly from the PC. Some are internal circuit boards, while others are external devices about the size of a videocassette (below). External modems plug into the back of the system unit, like the printer and monitor do.

Outside...

These components allow you to enter information into your PC, display what comes out and connect you to other PCs.

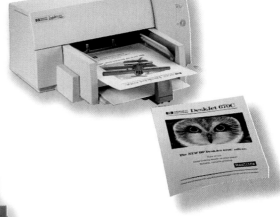

Printer

For home PC users, the ideal printer is the color inkjet (above), which can print color pictures and newsletters as well as traditional black and white letters. Laser printers (left) provide the best black and white printing quality.

Joystick

For many games, such as flight simulators, a joystick is almost essential. It works much like the control stick of an airplane.

Microphone

With a multimedia PC you can record your voice and sound effects on your computer. The microphone connects to the sound card, which converts the sound waves into numbers that the computer can store and replay at any time through the speakers.

A DIRECT LINE TO THE FUTURE

A multimedia PC, attached to a telephone line via a modem, can do the job of a telephone, answering machine and fax machine. But when you combine this with the versatility of multimedia and the growth of the Internet, the possibilities expand even further. For instance, when making international telephone calls you can use Internet telephone software that lets you talk to anyone anywhere on the Internet. With the simple addition of a few extras, you can also use your PC as a videophone via the Internet.

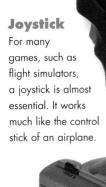

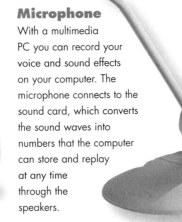

Mouse pad

It's a low-tech component, but don't forget it. A mouse pad makes your mouse easier to move and prolongs its working life (see page 91).

...and inside

If you understand the various component parts that have gone into producing your PC, you will have a much better idea of what you can get it to do.

System unit

The system unit is the most important part of the PC; inside are its 'brains'. Everything connects to the system unit – its back panel has sockets for all the external components shown on page 89. Some PCs have an all-in-one monitor and system unit.

Processor

This is the true brain of the PC and the most important component on the motherboard. It processes, understands and acts on the instruction contained in your software programs. Processors operate at speeds of several million instructions per second. Most processors in PCs are Intel Pentiums.

Memory

Every PC uses memory – special chips on the motherboard – as a high-speed workspace for the processor's calculations. When you start a program or open a letter, it is copied from the hard disk into the memory where the processor can work on it quickly. The more memory you have, the faster your PC will run. Memory is often referred to as **RAM**.

Motherboard

This is your PC's largest circuit board. All the internal components are either on the motherboard or connected to it. It has a bank of slots where you can plug in expansion cards, which are extra circuit boards that allow your PC to perform new tasks.

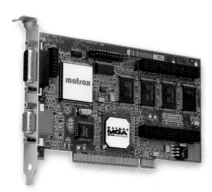

Graphics card

The graphics card (sometimes called the video card) shows on the screen the image that the processor has created in the memory. Sometimes the graphics card is built onto the motherboard, but often it's a separate expansion card (see Motherboard).

WHAT IT MEANS

RAM

RAM stands for Random Access Memory, although in practical terms it means memory that can be both read from and written to. This contrasts with Read Only Memory – ROM – from which you can read information, but not write to it.

Hard disk drive

Your PC needs somewhere to store long-term information because its memory literally goes blank when the PC is switched off. The hard disk provides a huge storage area for programs and documents that lasts as long as you want – even when the PC is turned off. The disk sits in an airtight metal box.

Sound card

The sound card sends the signal from the memory to the speakers when you want to hear sound from the PC. It can also play music from the CD-ROM drive through the speakers and convert sound from the microphone (see page 89).

Maintaining your mouse

Spare a thought for your hardworking mouse as you scroll around the Desktop. It takes a lot of punishment, but keep it clean and you'll be able to point with precision for a long time.

THE MOUSE is the main way you move around the computer screen. You use it to pick up and move files around the Desktop, scroll through documents, perform program commands and click on 'hotlinks' in Internet sites. Together with your keyboard, your mouse is a crucial way of communicating with your computer and therefore deserves some basic care.

Like any small device with moving parts, the mouse will not last forever. It can be simple and inexpensive to replace your mouse if it does suffer a fatal accident, but with sensible use and simple maintenance its working life can be greatly extended.

Your mouse will become 'sticky' as it picks up dirt during use. Make sure your PC is switched off before tackling your dirty mouse. There's no need to unplug the mouse from the computer, but this may make the process easier.

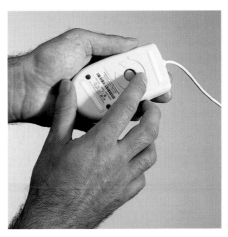

1 To remove surface grease and dirt, rub a mouse wipe gently but firmly all over the mouse's top and underside.

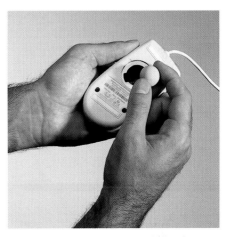

2 To clean the movable parts of the mouse, turn the mouse over and twist the circular plate counterclockwise a quarter turn.

3 When the plate is removed, turn the mouse over and the ball will fall out (hopefully into your hand).

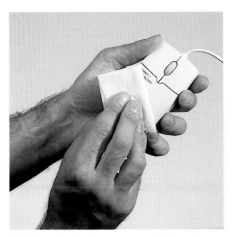

4 Clean the mouse ball first. Take a clean mouse wipe and, using the tips of your fingers and thumb, firmly rub the surface of the ball. The special wipes contain a solvent to help break down any dirt. You'll be amazed at the dirt that comes off the mouse ball.

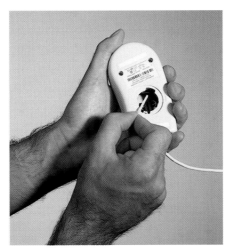

5 The biggest problems arise from the build-up of grime on the mouse's three internal rollers. Scrape the dirt from each of the rollers using a matchstick. Make sure that you remove all the dirt or you may find the mouse's movements are uneven when you use it again.

6 Reassemble the mouse by putting the ball back into the cavity and refitting the circular mouse plate. You'll get the most from your mouse if you clean it regularly. Keeping the area around your PC clean and using a mouse pad will reduce the amount of cleaning needed.

A tour around your keyboard

Shortcuts and hidden functions are just two of the secrets of your computer's keyboard. Find out more in this quick guided tour.

How well do you know your keyboard? Realize your PC's maximum potential by taking a little time to understand the keyboard's lesser-known keys.

The PC keyboard, with its 100 or so keys, is taken for granted by most people without a thought as to how it works, how it can be used more efficiently and how to look after it. Knowing all these things about your keyboard will help you get more from your home computing.

The heart of the keyboard is based on the typewriter layout that even two-finger typists recognize. However, in addition to the normal keys found on a typewriter, there is a numeric keypad that looks more like a calculator keyboard. This is useful when you type in lots of numbers. Don't let the missing multiplication and division signs throw you off – computer experts use [*] for multiply and [/] for divide. These are usually the middle two keys on the top row of the numeric keypad.

● Hit the right key

When you press a key, three things happen. The initial press of the key pushes two metal strips together to form an electrical connection. This tells the computer which key has been pressed. Then a spring under the key returns it to its upright position. Finally, the key makes a 'click' sound so that you know you have successfully pressed it, without having to look at the screen.

● A capital key

The best way of using your keyboard effectively is to learn a few of the shortcuts built into the software you use. These will involve multiple keystrokes, which means that you have to press two or three keys at once.

To get the hang of shortcuts, consider how you produce a capital (or upper case) letter in a document. Normally, pressing the [P] key produces a small (lower case) 'p'. To get a capital 'P', you must press [Shift] and [P].

Windows shortcuts use the [Ctrl] and the [Alt] keys, and you use them like the [Shift] key. For example, if you press [Alt]+[F4], the program or window you are using will close. [Ctrl]+[Esc] will bring up the Start menu at the bottom of your screen – even if you can't see the Start button.

Once you're used to shortcuts, you'll find Windows a lot quicker because you don't need to keep moving your hand away from the keyboard to the mouse and back.

CHECKPOINT

KEYBOARD CARE

☑ To clean your keyboard, turn the PC off, then wipe off any dirt with a slightly damp cloth. There might be dust and dirt trapped between the keys, so use a can of compressed air to blow the dust and dirt away.

☑ Keep food and drink away from the keyboard. A spilled drink can quickly render a keyboard useless.

☑ Prevention is better than cure. If, try as you might, you can't keep food and drink away, then use a keyboard seal. This is a plastic cover which protects your keyboard, but still lets you type. When it gets dirty, just pull it off and wash it.

The keys that unlock your PC

Some keys on your keyboard are more useful than you might think and a few of them are not much use at all! Here's what they all do.

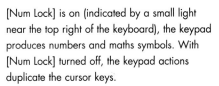

① [Esc] The Escape key is most often used to cancel the current menu or dialog box.

② [F1] The first of the function keys is usually used to summon up help in programs.

③ [F2] to [F12] The other function keys send commands to the software you are using to offer quick access to different options.

④ [Del] and [Backspace] Both keys delete a character: [Del] removes the one to the right of the cursor, [Backspace] removes one to the left.

⑤ The **[Print Screen], [Pause]** and the **[Scroll Lock]** keys (together with the **[Alt Gr]** key to the right of the spacebar) are almost redundant. Designed for 1980's software, they are rarely used by modern Windows programs.

⑥ Numeric keypad This has two functions controlled by the **[Num Lock]** key. When

[Num Lock] is on (indicated by a small light near the top right of the keyboard), the keypad produces numbers and maths symbols. With [Num Lock] turned off, the keypad actions duplicate the cursor keys.

⑦ [Home], [End], [Page Up] and **[Page Down]** These keys move you around your documents quickly.

⑧ Cursor keys These arrow keys move the cursor – the text insertion point in word processors, the cell highlighted in spreadsheets, etc. – around the screen.

⑨ Menu key Found on some Windows 95/98 keyboards, this shows the same menu you get by right-clicking the mouse button.

⑩ Windows logo Accesses the Start menu (on some Windows 95/98 keyboards only).

⑪ Spacebar Inserts a space between text characters (letters) in your documents.

⑫ [Shift], [Ctrl] and **[Alt]** These keys can be used with other keys to create shortcuts.

⑬ [Tab] This key adds spacing in documents. You can also use it to move around dialog boxes and the Windows Desktop.

The 'QWERTY' keyboard layout was inherited from typewriters. This strange layout was originally designed over a hundred years ago to slow typists down. With other layouts, fast typists could jam the typewriter!

Focus on your monitor

Your monitor can provide a high-quality sharp image, but to avoid straining your eyes, make sure that it's properly adjusted. It's not difficult to achieve a crystal-clear image when you know how.

Your monitor – the computer screen – is like a window through which you communicate with the computer. If you use the computer a lot, you may spend hours looking at the screen, so it's vital that it gives you the best possible picture.

Chances are that it might not be, especially if someone else set up the computer originally and it hasn't been adjusted since. It's often hard to tell if a computer monitor is set correctly, unless you know what to look for. However, since a poorly set up monitor contributes to fatigue and eyestrain, a few minutes spent adjusting the image are essential. Adjusting the picture – even cleaning the glass screen – can often make a spectacular improvement, and you should check that your monitor is set up to achieve the best possible picture quality.

● Cleaning
The monitor produces static electricity. That means it attracts fine dust like a magnet, and once it has been used for some time, the screen will have a coating of dust. Even though you can't see it easily, this dust will block the view. It acts to disperse light as it leaves the screen, and this leads to what looks like a fuzzy, or slightly out of focus, image.

● Adjusting picture quality
Unlike a TV, you can't change the color on most monitors, but you can adjust brightness and contrast. In addition to making sure that you can see the full range of light and dark detail in the image on your PC's screen, these controls can also affect how sharp the picture looks.

Most monitors have symbols to show which control is which: the

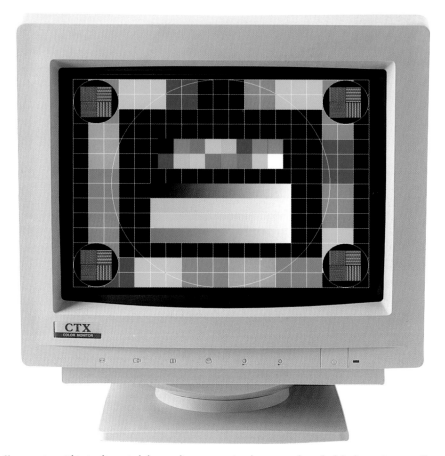

You can get special test software to help you adjust your monitor, but you can do much of the fine-tuning yourself by adjusting the image's brightness and contrast and making sure it fills the full area of the screen.

brightness control usually looks like a sun image – a circle with lines radiating from it – and the contrast control looks like a half filled-in circle. Some monitors have rotary knobs, others have sliders. Some use two buttons and an on-screen bar; on these, you press the buttons and the on-screen bar shrinks or grows to show the level (just like many TVs do with the volume control).

You should also adjust the size and position of the image: the Windows Desktop should fill as much of the screen as possible. If your Desktop has a large and ugly black border, you can adjust the monitor to stretch the image area to fit the screen.

PC TIPS

Your monitor might have a degauss button. You'll rarely need it but it's necessary if there's a discolored area on the screen (due to magnetic build up). Press the button to demagnetize the screen. You'll hear a slight thump, the image will wobble then settle again.

Improving your monitor's picture

Just like a television, your computer monitor has controls to adjust the picture. Make sure that you're treating your eyes to the best possible view by fine-tuning the image quality and its size and position.

1 Look for a set of controls for adjusting brightness and contrast. These may be plainly visible below the screen or hidden behind a panel. They might be sliders, buttons, knobs or edge-wheels, and should be labeled with a pair of symbols like this. The 'sun' symbol is the brightness control, the semicircle is the contrast.

2 Open up a word processor and type in some text. Turn up the brightness as far as it will go. The left and right edges of the screen will turn from black to slightly gray.

3 Now turn the brightness down until this gray glow just merges back into the black border. This makes sure that black areas in your screen image emit no light.

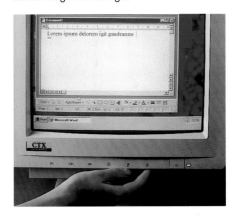

4 Now adjust the contrast to set the brightness of the white areas of the image. The picture is now at its optimum adjustment, and text should appear sharp.

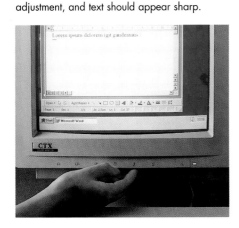

5 If your Desktop has a wide black border, look for a set of controls like these (once again, there are various kinds of control: knobs, buttons, etc). These are used to adjust picture size and position. Correct adjustment is very important or else shapes will appear odd: circles will look slightly squashed and squares will be rectangular, for example. Fill the screen fully and all your images will be displayed properly.

6 Use the controls to center the image on the screen. There is normally one control to move the image left and right, and another to move it up and down.

7 Use the size controls to stretch the image to fit the whole screen. A properly adjusted monitor will make your computer more pleasant – and less fatiguing – to use.

Cleaning and adjusting your screen

Use a glass-cleaning spray to clean the screen, making sure the monitor is switched off. Spray a little cleaner on a soft cloth (never on the monitor itself) and wipe the glass. The cloth will probably become a dirty black color. Repeat this cleaning until the cloth is clean.

Make sure that the screen is adjusted to the most comfortable angle on its tilt-and-swivel adjusters. As well as pointing toward you, angle the monitor so it doesn't catch the reflection from a window or a room light, as this will make it hard to see the display.

Bits and bytes

Computer equipment – from memory to modems to hard disks – is always measured in bits and bytes. If you've ever wondered what this jargon really means, read on.

However big the hard disk on your PC, as you use your computer and install new software, you'll probably find it fills up surprisingly quickly. Most PC users quickly learn that it pays to manage storage efficiently and to keep an eye on how much space is left on their hard disks.

Computer storage is mainly measured in bytes, kilobytes (KB), megabytes (MB) and gigabytes (GB). There are 1,024 bytes in a kilobyte, 1,024KB in a megabyte and 1,024MB in a gigabyte. The table above right will help you put the numbers in perspective: think of a byte as a single letter (A, B, etc); modern hard disks can store over 20,000,000,000 of them.

● **Storing information**

Each byte is made up of even tinier units, called bits. These are the most fundamental building blocks, the smallest possible pieces of computer information. Effectively, a bit is like a switch: it can be either on or off. In the binary code that all computers use, this is expressed as either a 1 or a 0 – hence the name bit, which is short for Binary digIT.

A bit is so small that it doesn't mean much on its own. But add it to other bits and the computer can recognize the combination as a code for a number or letter. It takes eight bits to make a unit of information, one byte. As a useful reminder, think of byte as BinarY digiT Eight.

As a ready reckoner, 1KB is roughly equal to half a page of typed text. You can see how adding letters and words to your documents affects file sizes by following the step-by-step exercise on the opposite page.

In fact, as the table above shows, programs often take up most of your hard disk, and it's because of their size that the CD-ROM drive was introduced. CD-ROMs can store large amounts of information – such as interactive encyclopedias – without filling up your hard disk drive.

It's important to avoid completely filling up your hard disk. Try to keep at least five percent free at all times. We looked at the basics of file management on pages 18–21.

Exploring the size of your documents

Follow these straightforward steps to see the relationship between the amount of information contained in your documents and the amount of hard disk space used to store them.

1 Use the mouse to move the cursor on the My Computer icon, which is usually in the top left-hand corner of your screen. Click twice on it with the left mouse button.

2 When the My Computer window opens, use the mouse to click twice on the computer hard disk icon labeled (C:).

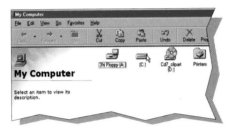

3 Another window will open, which shows the folders and files on your hard disk (the exact contents depend on the software installed on your PC's hard disk). Look for the folder called My Documents. If you can't see all the folders, use the scroll bars to move your view of the window. Double-click on the My Documents folder with the left mouse button.

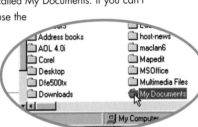

4 You'll see the My Documents window (its contents will depend on the files you have previously saved into this folder). Click on View on the Menu bar and then click on the Details command from the drop-down menu.

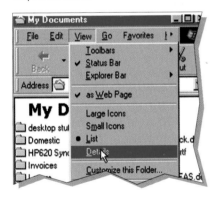

5 You will see a list of your files with – from left to right – an icon of the program used to create the file, its title, its size in kilobytes (KB), the file type and the date the file was last modified.

6 Some files are bigger than others. This is partly to do with how many words they contain, but files containing pictures will be much bigger than text-only files. Generally, the more you add, the larger a file gets. To see this, open one of the files you can see in your My Documents window. We've chosen 'bankletter.doc', which Windows tells us has a file size of 21KB. When the document is loaded and before you do anything else, move the cursor up to the File menu and select Save As.

7 In the Save As dialog box that pops up, type a new name for the file (we've called it 'Demo.doc') and click on the Save button on the right-hand side of the box. The reason for doing this is to make sure that the original 'bankletter.doc' file is safe and intact – we can work on 'Demo.doc' without worrying about changing the original.

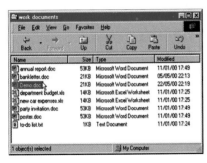

8 Type in several new paragraphs (we've copied the first paragraph several times). Select Save from the File menu and close the program. Return to the My Documents window (if necessary, by repeating steps 1–2 above).

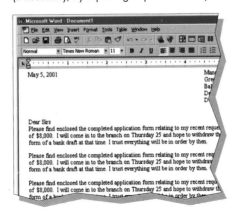

9 Compare the file sizes: our 'Demo.doc' is 11KB bigger than the old one, 'bankletter.doc' – 32KB instead of 21KB.

PC TIPS

To check how much hard disk space you have left, double-click on the My Computer icon, then click once on the (C:) icon. The amount of free space is shown in the middle section of the window's Status bar.

Choosing a printer

Printers are important pieces of hardware – they let you see the documents you have created on paper. You can then check your work and print out as many copies as you need. As with other PC accessories, the right choice of printer depends on what you want to use it for.

In the past, PC users had little choice when it came to printers. Nowadays, there are scores to choose from, and the prices vary considerably. At the bottom of the printer cost range are low-cost but slow color inkjet printers. At the top are professional laser printers giving razor-sharp printouts in full color. In between, there is a range of options, but unless you're working on a tight budget, the choice you have to make is between a color inkjet printer designed for the home market or a laser printer for quality black-and-white work.

● A question of quality

Although color inkjet printers can be sluggish and produce less-than-sharp print, they can turn out dazzling posters, photographs and letters in full color, making them ideal for family use. Moderately priced laser printers, on the other hand, give only black and white, but are quick and produce top-quality printouts, making them ideal for anyone running a business from home. Let's have a look at these two types of printer.

● Inkjet printers

Recent advances in inkjet printing technology mean that quality full-color printing is now within the reach of every home PC user. Inkjet printers work by heating ink in the printhead so that a bubble forms and forces an ink droplet out of a nozzle – the inkjet. Some use a piezoelectric 'pump' instead, but the effect is the same – to force a jet of ink out onto the paper. The nozzle has to be very fine – finer even than a human

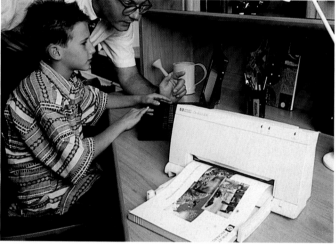

A color inkjet is the best all-round family choice unless you also need a printer to run a business from home.

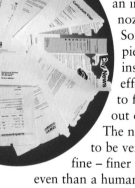

Most inkjet printers give printouts in full color, as well as black and white.

hair – to produce the detail needed for quality printing.

There is one set of jets for each of the different colored inks. Strangely, the color is made by using inks of just three colors: cyan (a kind of blue-green), magenta (purple-red) and yellow. By using the inks together, the printer can create most colors of the rainbow. The reservoirs for these three inks and the printhead are combined in the inkjet cartridge.

Most inkjet printers have a second cartridge containing a reservoir of black ink for high-quality text printing. A few low-cost printers have only one cartridge and mix the cyan, magenta and yellow inks to make black, but print quality for text documents is generally poor with such printers.

● Inkjet limitations

The inkjet cartridges must be replaced when the ink runs out, and they can be expensive to buy because many

---

PC TIPS

When buying a printer – and especially a color inkjet – ask to see samples of the printouts it can produce on plain paper. Beware of choosing a printer on the basis of its print quality on expensive coated paper only. If you are buying a printer for the first time, remember to get a printer cable. Manufacturers might not include them, and they're essential.

include part of the printer's electronics. Ink refill kits cut the cost.

Inkjet printers can also be fussy about the paper they need. While ordinary copier paper is acceptable for text and simple illustrations, the best photo-quality printouts call for specially coated paper, which can be quite expensive. The coating is designed to produce clean, full colors with little or no paper wrinkling.

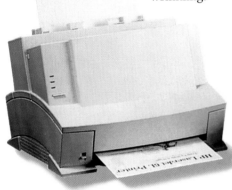

Laser printers will give the professional quality you need for most black-and-white documents and images.

Photographs printed on plain copier paper often look dull and have little contrast. It is important not to be too ambitious with home color inkjets. Low printing speeds and the high page costs of coated paper make it impractical to run off large quantities of color prints on an inkjet printer. Just six copies of a letter-size full-color print will cost between $3 and $7 to produce and take anywhere from 15 to 30 minutes to print. The other disadvantage of color inkjet printing is the fragility of the print. It can smear, especially when damp.

PRINTER PRICES

Always shop around when you are thinking about buying a printer. Prices will vary considerably among dealers – even for the same model.
• A color inkjet printer costs around $75-150.
• Black-and-white laser printers cost around $200-400.
• If your budget is tight, you can get a lower-resolution color inkjet printer for as little as $40.

● Laser printers

If you don't need color, but want the very best black-and-white print quality, there is only one choice: the laser printer. These print out high-quality documents quickly, and you can print on a wide range of paper sizes, labels and other formats. The printouts from a laser printer are also more robust than those from an inkjet; they are actually waterproof.

Personal laser printers for the home work exactly the same way as their professional cousins. A laser beam scans across an electrically charged cylinder (called a drum) leaving a pattern of dots to which toner (ink) particles stick. Once transferred onto the paper, heat melts the toner in place.

Laser printers can print several thousand sheets before the toner runs out. When it does, you simply buy a new cartridge. On most laser printers, the cartridge includes the drum, and replacements can be quite expensive. A few laser printers use separate drum

Despite the high initial purchase price, laser printers can be economical to run if they are used sensibly.

and toner cartridges. These can be cheaper to run, as you rarely need to change the drum and the toner cartridge is cheaper.

One important laser-printer feature to look for is an energy-saving mode. This means the printer automatically goes into a standby mode if you don't use it for a while, so you can leave your printer on all the time. It can take a while for the printer to 'wake up' again when you do print, but you'll save electricity and the printer will usually run quieter in the energy-saving mode, too.

Whatever printer you ultimately decide on, there are several features to check out. Try to anticipate the type and volume of printing you'll be doing when you consider these points:

☑ Speed
The printing speed is measured in pages per minute (which you'll often see abbreviated to ppm). This is one of the most important aspects of the printer if you will be turning out lots of pages. Six or eight pages per minute is usual for personal laser printers. Inkjets usually run at about half that speed.

For the very best color print quality, check out high resolution (720dpi or more) color inkjets.

☑ Print quality
Print quality depends largely on resolution. Resolution is measured in dots per inch (or dpi) and is simply the number of dots the printer can print in each inch. With more dots per inch, the printer can produce finer detail in pictures and sharper text for letters. The cheapest printers produce 300dpi, while more expensive models manage 600dpi. Some color inkjets achieve 720dpi or even 1440dpi on special paper. 300dpi is fine for general home use, but for home-business use, 600dpi is best.

☑ Paper handling
Not all printers cope well with envelopes, labels and special printing needs. On the whole, laser printers are more flexible. Their input tray holds more pages, many can print on very thick paper and most take single manually fed sheets – useful for printing an occasional sheet of letter-headed paper without removing all the plain paper. On the other hand, inkjets can print on types of letter-headed paper which llasers cannot (due to the heating process), and some can print on continuous paper for banners.

Perfect printing

For most home computer users, a color inkjet printer is the ideal choice – they are simple to use, versatile and, if you follow a few basic tips, reasonably inexpensive to run. Over the next few pages we show you how to get more from your printer.

Your printer will give you great results even if all you do is click the print button and never delve deeper into its capabilities. However, to really get the most out of your printer – the very best print quality and the optimum use of paper and ink – a little experimentation goes a long way.

● Before you buy

All you need to set up your home print shop are a printer, a cable to connect it to your PC and paper to use in your printer. If you haven't selected a printer yet, consider what you will use it for to guide you to the one best suited to your needs.

There are almost as many different uses of a printer as there are printers to choose from – it's up to you to decide what you want to do: write letters, make greetings cards, print photographs or design menus.

If you expect to be producing a lot of printed sheets, then the cost per page and printing speed are both important points to consider. Be wary of those less expensive printers that have only one cartridge instead of the more usual combination of one black ink and one color ink cartridge

(see pages 98–99). These can turn out to be a false economy, as they must create black by blending colors, a process that can be wasteful. Look for a store that will print test pages for the various

Some printers come with software, such as 101 Dalmatians Print Studio, to capitalize on popular films and help teach children the basics of printing.

printers. You'll then have some hard facts to help in your decision.

Some inkjet printers come with great family-oriented software. Shop around and you'll find printers that can print transfers for your own T-shirt designs and models that can print on continuous paper so you can make long banners. Some printers come with software aimed specifically at children and the home user. Disney's Print Studio and Windows Draw 6 SE are ideal ways to start.

● Photographic quality

For more general letter-size printing, most inkjet printers are capable of turning out impressive, almost photographic, quality images. This opens possibilities for all sorts of customized family albums and

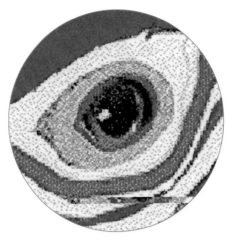

The quality and detail that can be achieved with today's inkjet printers are stunning. Here's an almost photographic quality printout from a Hewlett-Packard inkjet printer. The picture on the left is shown at actual size. On the right, we've zoomed right in to show the details of the dots that make up the image.

local office supplier and ask about stocks of colored paper. You'll find plain paper in various colors, as well as blank certificates, sheets of labels, business cards and color designs. With a few lines of printing from your inkjet, these pages could look just as good as if you had printed the whole thing on plain white paper.

With imagination, you should be able to turn these blanks into party invitations, birthday and Christmas cards, club membership cards and menus. Using these ready-made blanks, you win several times over: you save money on ink, you save on design time and you also save print time because you're only printing your own color graphics, not the whole page.

birthday cards. When you print photographs you'll find that the quality of paper makes a big difference for the final result.

● Hidden costs

A color inkjet may be cheap to buy, but there are hidden costs behind the sales talk. The claims of hundreds of sheets of printing from a single color cartridge must be considered with caution. If you try to print full-page, full-color pictures, you'll find that the

ink runs out long before. Such figures are usually based on just 15 per-cent color ink on a page. This is reasonable for text pages with small color graphics, but if you intend to print full-page designs, expect the life of your color cartridge to be somewhat shorter.

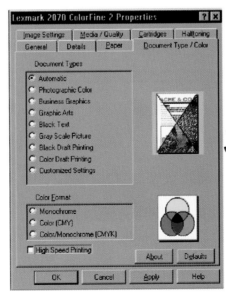

Printouts from inkjets like this Hewlett-Packard DeskJet 880C look stunning, but make sure you keep paper and ink costs under control.

● Software control

The printer software is the key to getting the most from your printer. This is the software that lets your other programs control the printer. With the software, you can alter paper size and type and select the print quality you need. For the best results you can opt for fast, but lesser quality draft mode or slower presentation mode.

● Printing on color

If you want to produce pages with a solid color background, then visit a

Normally, when you print – from a word processor, for example – you just press the OK button in the Print dialog box to send your document to the printer. If you press the Properties button beforehand, you'll see a printer control page like this one. Explore your printer's Print Properties dialog box; you might spot capabilities that you missed in the printer's manual. This Hewlett-Packard DeskJet printer, for example, can print on continuous paper to make banners.

Most Print Properties dialog boxes let you set the type of print job. The printer will then subtly alter the way the page is printed to produce the best possible quality.

Experimenting with your printer

Color printers are great fun, but to make sure you don't waste time, ink and paper, you'll need to take the guesswork out of printing. Here's how to create your own reference pages to show what your printer can do.

GETTING THE best results out of your printer is a lot easier when you have a good idea of the full range of results this piece of hardware can actually deliver. For example, what types of print jobs benefit from special paper? Is plain copier paper suitable for printing children's paintings? Which typefaces will look best for the club newsletter?

By spending a little time creating some test pages, you'll have a ready reference to help you answer these questions. The following exercises will teach you more about your printer and help take the guesswork out of color printing.

● Test different types of paper
You can use Word to create sample pages that are representative of the types of documents you print. If you use colorful WordArt, clip art and/or your own graphics (see pages 44–47), be sure to add them to your samples. Try to fit them on to one page to save paper.

Now print this page on a selection of different paper types (your printer manual will tell you which types of paper your printer can use). You'll need to buy some sheets of each type to do this, but the investment is well worth it. Look closely at the print quality for each type of object on

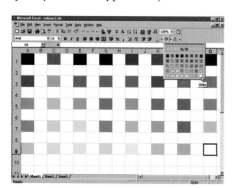

Try using Excel to make a simple color swatch page – just color each cell. Copy the layout of the drop-down color palette so you know which color is which.

You can create a font reference document to show all the fonts on your PC. You'll be able to see more detail in the printed letters than you can on your computer screen.

your page. Try to get a feel for which type of paper is worth the extra investment and which is not.

Clearly name each paper type and store this print file by your printer so that whenever you need to print something out of the ordinary, you can simply pull out the file and find the best paper to use.

● Compile a font list
It's important to make sure that you choose the right font (typeface) for the job. Here's how to print your own font guide: open Word and type in the names of the fonts listed in the font box, one font to a line. Now select each line in turn, and change the font to correspond with its name (see pages 34–35).

Again, print out the page and store it in your print file. When you need to create something special, you can make sense of all these font names at a glance. You'll find that it's a lot easier to select fonts from your printed page than you can from the computer screen.

● Create a color swatch
The biggest area of guesswork comes when you print colors. Computer screens and inkjet printer colors rarely match perfectly because they work in very different ways.

To remove the guesswork, print a color swatch page. You can use this like the paint booklets you get from DIY stores. With a single page of color squares to choose from, you can choose colors with confidence.

Many Windows programs have a basic palette of around 40 colors. You can use Excel to create a grid of squares with a different color in each (see pages 56–57). This will provide a simple guide; print it on the different types of paper to see how the paper quality affects the color. Add these pages to your printer reference file.

If you haven't got Excel, use Paint. You can draw rectangles in colors from the palette at the bottom of the Paint window (see pages 62–63).

DOs AND DON'Ts

DO keep a page count of black-and-white printouts and a color page count. You can then discover the real costs of running your printer.

DO try out various papers to find the best one for you. Different papers produce surprisingly varied results.

DO experiment with the printer settings. This will help you to find the right balance between print quality, cost and print speed.

DO maintain your printer regularly by following the advice given in your printer's manual.

DON'T believe on-screen colors – use your color test swatch.

DON'T waste paper and ink – use draft-mode printing until you are sure your document is 100 percent correct.

Adding a printer to your PC

Don't be put off by the task of adding a printer to your system. With this guide and the helpfulness of Windows, you'll quickly be up and running.

Once you have selected the printer, its icon appears in the Printers folder. The check mark indicates that it has been selected as the default printer.

ONCE YOU'VE bought your printer, you're only a few steps away from printing your first pages.

● Unpack
First, remove the printer and its accessories from its packing material. Keep the cardboard shapes and tape used to hold the printer parts in position while in transit.

● Find space
Now find a location that's close enough to connect the printer to your PC and also accessible enough for adding and removing paper.

● Insert paper and cartridge(s)
Place some paper in the printer. Then connect the printer power supply and follow the printer manual's instructions for inserting the inkjet or laser printer cartridges. For the moment, keep your computer switched off.

● Connect the printer to the PC
The physical connections are easy to follow. Check our guide (Connecting the printer and computer, below) to see exactly what goes where.

● Switch on
First turn the printer on, then your computer. This makes sure that Windows can try to automatically detect the new printer. A message will appear on your screen, asking for the software for the printer. Insert the disks provided along with your printer as they are requested.

If Windows doesn't spot your new printer, the printer manual will show you how to install the software.

● Print test page
When all the steps have been carried out, Windows will ask you if you want to print out a test page. Click on the OK button, and your printer will now start working.

● Set default printer
Click the Yes button when Windows asks you if you want the printer to be the default printer. This makes sure that your printed pages go directly to this printer without requiring further intervention from you.

● Restart the computer
Restart Windows, and you'll be able to use your new printer right away.

Connecting the printer and computer

Connecting a printer to your computer is easy: there's only one cable and it fits only one way, so you don't need to worry about making any mistakes. Here's your guide to trouble-free printer connection.

STEP-BY-STEP PRINTER CONNECTION

1. Make sure that your computer is switched off. Plug the printer power cable into the wall outlet and the power socket into the printer.
2. Connect the computer and the printer using the printer cable – sometimes called a parallel cable. There is only one way to do this: look at the connectors on each end of the cable and you'll see the difference.
3. At the printer end, the cable's larger plug fits into the slot, which may have two metal clips. Connect it and secure it with the clips.
4. Only one computer socket will match the other end of the printer cable. This socket will be marked, perhaps with a printer icon, or the label 'LPT1'. Connect the printer cable and tighten the two screws to secure it.
5. Switch on the printer first, and then the computer. Here's how it should look (above).

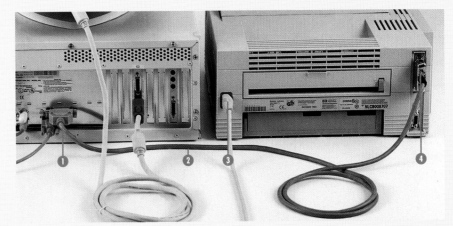

❶ The socket for the printer cable is always at the rear of the computer, close to the other sockets. It's fairly easy to spot because PCs have only one socket of this type.
❷ The printer cable should be long enough to allow flexibility in printer placement.

❸ This printer uses a standard power cord for its power supply. Some others – mainly inkjets – use an external adaptor.
❹ The other end of the printer cable plugs into the printer and may be held in place by two metal clips to secure a good connection.

Home Learning & Leisure

Choosing your software

Selecting home learning software is a tricky business because there are so many titles on the market. So what should you look for when you go out to buy your educational programs?

Your PC is superb for home learning, but however impressive your hardware, it's useless without good software. There are three basic types of home learning software: reference, study and edutainment.

CD-ROMs store vast amounts of information, so reference software, such as Microsoft's *Encarta Encyclopedia 2001* (see pages 108–109) and Dorling Kindersley's *Chronicle of the 20th Century*, nearly always come in this format.

Whereas books deliver text and pictures only, software resources like these provide a multimedia experience, with extras like sound, video and interactive features. However, it's important that you are able to find your way to the facts you want without too much trouble, so look for a title with a powerful but simple-to-use search engine.

Value for money is important when assessing software. Programs aren't cheap, so look for depth of content and different levels of complexity.

OUT THERE

A wide selection of home-learning software is available from computer superstores as well as other specialist outfits. Most software companies will also supply software directly to their customers via mail order – if you find one type of program is particularly suited to your family's needs, why not contact the publisher to get a catalogue of its other titles?

The majority of software makers have websites and, if you have Internet access, you can check details, download demonstration versions and buy the software online.

The hallmark of good educational software is an ability to make the learning experience enjoyable, not only for the student, but for the whole family. Look for software that uses all the advantages of multimedia and interactivity that the home computer can bring.

● **Study software**
Study software is designed to help you learn a subject or develop a specific skill. An example includes the keyboard tutor, *Mavis Beacon Teaches Typing* (see pages 112–113). There is software, too, to help with tests and exams.

This type of software usually relies on a degree of repetition, but the key is whether the exercises are fun, so look out for programs that give feedback to the user through test results and advice on areas where further practice is needed.

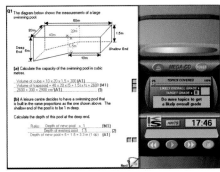

Educational software is available for all age groups. This example is aimed at teenagers. Not only does it feature interactive exercise sheets, but a character called Dan the Man hands out practical advice for exam candidates, such as preparing a revision timetable and avoiding stress during exam time.

● Edutainment software

Edutainment software aims to entertain as well as educate. For instance, *Professor Tim* (Sierra) is a science package that features puzzles based around the professor's workshop. As well as being fun, it teaches children about scientific principles, and they then have to apply that knowledge to solve the puzzles. When choosing this type of program, look for a balance between learning and enjoyment.

Most software boasts that it is interactive, but real interactivity is more than just clicking on-screen buttons. Programs should encourage children to get involved in the content by giving them an opportunity to use their own creative abilities, or by providing follow-up activities. With Enid Blyton's *Noddy* (Cedant Multimedia), for example, children

Software can be expensive, so put plenty of thought into the type you want and consider whether it is suitable for your intended uses and the type of computer you have.

can follow the stories, turning the pages of an interactive storybook and clicking on words to hear how they are pronounced. They can also create a Toytown scene, thereby developing their technology and design skills.

● Looking good

Any software, whether for children or adults, has to be visually stimulating. It is important to investigate the quality of the graphics (sometimes they are enhanced on the packaging so what you see isn't necessarily what you get). If children find software boring, they won't use it. If you're

buying a book you can flip through it to see whether it's suitable, but software comes in shrink-wrapped boxes, so you can't examine it in the same way. However, it's worth asking for an in-store demonstration or, better still, ask friends who have computers to show you packages that their children enjoyed so you can try before you buy.

*Aimed at three- to six-year-olds, Enid Blyton's **Noddy** has a variety of interactive features, such as using characters and stickers to create a Toytown scene.*

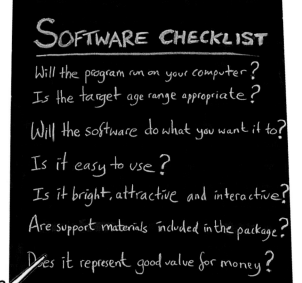

SOFTWARE CHECKLIST

Will the program run on your computer?

Is the target age range appropriate?

Will the software do what you want it to?

Is it easy to use?

Is it bright, attractive and interactive?

Are support materials included in the package?

Does it represent good value for money?

Can you try before you buy?

Facts at your fingertips

A single CD-ROM encyclopedia can store all the information you would expect to find in a multivolume printed set – with the added bonus of sound, videos and animation.

When was the last time you looked at a printed encyclopedia, reading articles and studying the pictures and tables? If you can't remember, you're like most people. After an initial flurry of use, encyclopedias are usually placed on a bookshelf and left to gather dust.

Part of the reason for this is that encyclopedias contain huge amounts of information. They're perfect when you want to look up something specific, but if you want to read more about a topic, you can spend a lot of time wading through the index, flicking through pages and cross-referencing other volumes in the series. Often, more time is spent looking for information than digesting it!

● CD-ROMs to the rescue

Enter the CD-ROM – a disc similar to the audio CDs you buy in music stores. Instead of just storing music, however, the CD-ROM contains text, pictures, graphics and sound that can all be accessed on your PC.

WHAT HARDWARE?

The CD-ROMs featured opposite will work on most multimedia PCs that have a CD-ROM drive, 256-color display, sound card and speakers. You'll probably need at least 16, or possibly 32, megabytes of memory on your PC (a megabyte is a measure of computer memory). Make sure to check the minimum requirements on the CD-ROM box before you buy.

CD-ROMs make ideal storage systems for encyclopedias because they can hold vast amounts of information. They are well worth their cost and can be used again and again, whenever your child has a new homework topic, or when you need to look something up yourself. What's more, because they are interactive, CD-ROMs make learning an enjoyable experience for children.

Traditional leatherbound encyclopedias face strong competition from one of the most exciting developments in home learning – the CD-ROM encyclopedia. These discs contain huge amounts of visual and written information that can be explored at the click of the mouse button. They also make searching for information easy.

● An encyclopedia for the family

Microsoft's *Encarta Encyclopedia 2001* is the latest version of one of the best-known CD-ROM encyclopedias. It has more than 32,000 articles, covering topics from the arts, sports, history and religion, through to current events and more, with cross-referencing to make searching easy. There are also over 100 video clips, 3,500 sound clips and 7,000 images.

When you start *Encarta*, the Home screen displays a Pinpointer panel that lets you search the whole database. Just type a word or phrase into the Find box and press [Enter]. *Encarta* displays the full list of matches on the left – just click on an entry to go to that page.

The Millennium Trails button on the Home screen lets you review the last millennium in a number of subjects – from literature through human endeavor to science. Choose your subject and a Topic Trails window links together articles that illustrate progress and change over the last thousand years.

Encarta is suitable for secondary school pupils and college students, as well as fact-hungry adults. Young children will love seeing a spider spin its web and hearing 60 languages spoken. There are also games and interactive features to enjoy.

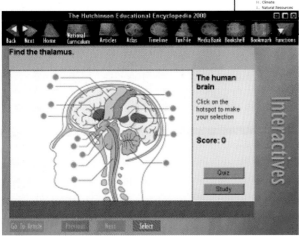

Encarta uses pictures, text and animation to make the learning experience more enjoyable. The pages are packed with links so that you can easily 'read around' a topic.

The colorful screen of the Hutchinson Educational Encyclopedia lets you explore articles, time lines, an atlas and a wide range of topics related to school curriculums.

● Knowledge in depth

Sometimes CD-based encyclopedias can appear a bit lightweight. They might be full of pictures and video clips, but if you want to investigate a particular interest in depth, they can be disappointing. If you're looking for something with more pedigree and heavyweight coverage, try *Encyclopedia Britannica 2001*, the CD-ROM version of the *Encyclopedia Britannica*, a respected source of knowledge since 1768.

The *Encyclopedia Britannica 2001* is a truly vast resource, containing more than 80,000 articles and 10,000 photographs, interactive maps, video clips and animations. It also includes the *New Dictionary of English* to help you improve your word power, and can direct you to websites for further research.

Those familiar with the Internet will notice how similar *Britannica*'s opening screen is to a website (it actually uses a version of Netscape Navigator as a search engine). Don't be put off by this comparison if you know nothing about the Web, because *Britannica* is very user-friendly. You can type in natural language sentences such as 'How many legs does a centipede have?' and it will provide you with a list of search results, with articles ranked in order of relevance. This is good, college-level research material for people who want more than soundbites of information.

INFORMATION SEARCH

With a little bit of practice, you will soon learn how to find what you want easily and quickly. These reference CD-ROMs have simple search interfaces, where you key in a topic and let your computer do the hard work of searching through data. However, if you can't find what you're looking for immediately, don't give up. Double-click on the main entry and you will bring up a list of subtopics. Often you will find multimedia elements such as sound clips, photographs and video sequences. Most encyclopedias also have links to relevant websites.

Increase your word power

When you are preparing a document on your computer and want to check up on any of the words, you can have instant access to a wealth of detailed reference material – at the touch of a key.

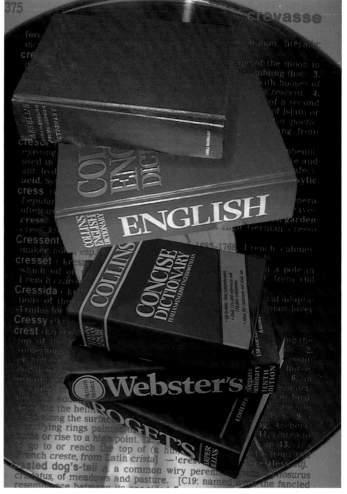

Few books that we use frequently are as useful as a dictionary – and few are as bulky. The more detailed they are, the heavier they are, and the longer you might have to spend looking for what you're after. But it doesn't have to be like that; with a software dictionary or other reference work, all your information fits on one CD-ROM. Browsing and searching is thus faster and more convenient.

You might be used to running the spell-checker over any documents you write in Word and you might even have tried Word's thesaurus function to search for new or different words to use (we will cover these Word functions later in the course). But while these functions are fine for ensuring the accuracy of documents, reference CD-ROMs do much more. Not only will they help your spelling,

they can also tell you the definition and origins of a word and lead you to quotes, facts and other information to inspire and inform you. With a good reference CD-ROM at your fingertips, you will never be at a loss for words again.

● A Desktop bookshelf

Microsoft *Bookshelf* 99 is one such comprehensive collection of good and quick to use reference resources. It includes the following: the full text of the *Columbia Dictionary of Quotations*; the *American Heritage Dictionary; World Almanac and Book of Facts; The People's Chronology;* and *Roget's Thesaurus,* to help you find the right word for the right occasion; and an Internet directory of nearly 5,000 useful reference sites.

The Microsoft Bookshelf Reference Collection is more than just a CD-ROM dictionary. For example, you might start with a simple question about the spelling of 'Churchill', but your inquiry will lead you to a wealth of biographical and historical information about this famous politician and his life.

All these words might seem a little daunting, but *Bookshelf* makes the information much more accessible by presenting it in an exciting way. When you search for a word, you get not only its spelling and meaning, but also a complete list of all the references available in *Bookshelf*. These appear down the side of the screen, color coded to show in which section they can be found.

Look up the spelling of the name 'Churchill', for instance, and you can quickly see biographical details of the famous British prime minister, listen to a recording of one of his well-known wartime speeches, or browse through quotations by and about him. With its dynamic use of sound, video and animation, *Bookshelf* is a true multimedia resource that should appeal to a wide range of age groups.

● An Oxford education

The *Oxford Reference Shelf*, on the other hand, is aimed at the older, perhaps more serious user. It makes few concessions to multimedia

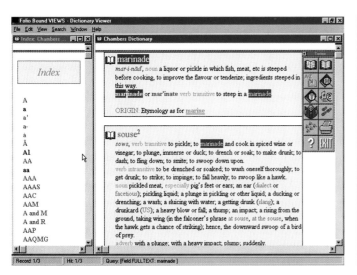

Several dictionaries are available as stand-alone programs (without any additional encyclopedia or multimedia software) to enhance your word power and knowledge.

The Dorling Kindersley Children's Dictionary is much more attractive to look at than the adult alternatives. Children can listen to the words as well as read them.

and contains no sound or images. Instead, it concentrates on delivering a mass of high-quality information in a fast and accessible way. The *Oxford Reference Shelf* contains no fewer than 16 different books, including dictionaries, encyclopedias and thesauruses.

● A basic dictionary

Not everyone wants these multi-volume reference works, however. If you are just looking for a dictionary that you can dip into at the click of a mouse, The *Concise Oxford Dictionary* is available as a

stand-alone reference work – as is its rival, the *Chambers Dictionary*. Both CD-ROMs have clear, simple screens that make searching for words a straightforward and easy procedure.

The Concise Oxford Dictionary CD-ROM does the thumbing of pages for you, quickly finding the word you're looking for.

● Kids' reference

The reference works mentioned so far are aimed at the adult user. Children, however, are not neglected, and two CD-ROMs from Dorling Kindersley cover ages from three up to 12.

My First Incredible Amazing Dictionary comes in a package filled with a range of activity material for children between three and seven years old. The CD-ROM itself is a bright and breezy lexicon of 1,000 words, all illustrated and with spoken sound recordings. The CD-ROM works in a simple enough way for young children to master without much parental

intervention. There are also several rewarding word games to test what children have learned while they've been using the CD-ROM.

The printed part of the package includes educational games with animal stickers to match up to words as well as a fun treasure hunt.

The Dorling Kindersley *Children's Dictionary* is for older children, aged from seven to 12. This also has lots of sound and animation. For example, select a letter and you get a screen full of objects that animate when you click on them. There's also an entertaining version of charades. However, the core of the CD-ROM is the list of 14,500 words with fully explained definitions – children can just type in a word to search for, or simply learn as they browse.

SITES TO @ VISIT

Yahoo!
www.yahoo.com
Yahoo! has divided its reference sites into different subject areas, such as Computing, Language and Science, so choose the one you think is the best match.

Dorling Kindersley
www.dk.com
Visit this site to find out more about the Dorling Kindersley CD-ROMs, *My First Incredible Amazing Dictionary* and the *Children's Dictionary*.

Microsoft
www.bookshelf.msn.com
This site will give you more information about Microsoft's *Bookshelf*.

Dorling Kindersley's colorful My First Incredible Amazing Dictionary will capture the imagination of children ages three to seven.

Teach yourself to type

Typing properly makes using your PC less tiring and increases the speed of your work. And with the help of your PC you don't need to go to evening classes to increase your words-per-minute speed.

Not so long ago, typing was considered a secretarial skill and primarily the domain of women. How times have changed. Today, everyone from a preschool child to a top executive in a multinational business has to type when they come into contact with a computer.

Most people are self-taught two-finger typists, and although many two-finger typists can achieve good speeds, most still have to search the keyboard for the letters they want – 'hunt and peck', as it is called.

● **Get your ideas down**
Strangely, a lot of people still regard touch-typing as something needed only to be a copy typist. And because copy typing is still thought of as a secretarial task, learning to touch-type is a skill many computer users dismiss. This is a mistake. For one thing, no matter what you are writing, be it a school essay, a business report or a chapter of your long-awaited novel, trying to get your thoughts down on paper isn't easy. How often have you had the exact words you need come

As computers are used in more aspects of our work and home lives, it is becoming ever more worthwhile to learn proper keyboard skills. Fortunately, your home PC makes a perfect teacher.

into your head and then fly straight out again, to disappear forever, while you have been searching for the correct keys?

What matters is getting the words, sentences and paragraphs down – not forgetting them as you search the keyboard for 'K' or 'A'. But even if you don't need to type quickly, touch-typing is often more accurate, less stressful and less likely to cause the keyboard-related RSI, or Repetitive Strain Injury.

If you want to learn to type properly, where better to learn than seated at your own PC? There are lots

of typing tutors to help you and they needn't cost you an arm and a leg. In fact, there are some excellent tutors available as shareware.

● **Learning with Mavis**
Queen among the typing tutors is Mavis Beacon. *Mavis Beacon Teaches Typing* is considered to be one of the best typing courses, on or off the computer, and even expert

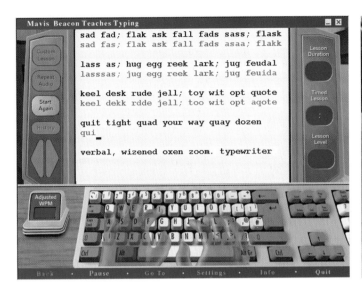

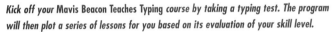

Kick off your **Mavis Beacon Teaches Typing** *course by taking a typing test. The program will then plot a series of lessons for you based on its evaluation of your skill level.*

There is a huge range of exercises in Mavis Beacon, *covering all the keyboard skills. This lesson practices the vital technique of finger positioning.*

typists can use the program to improve their skills. Personal lessons are designed especially for you on the basis of the results of a test and your answers to questions about your age and typing proficiency.

The course covers everything you would expect to find in a classroom, but you have the advantage of working at your own speed and the ability to repeat the lessons as often as you like until you are ready to move on. You will also get spoken feedback and encouragement from Mavis.

There are eight arcade-style games to provide a break from the lessons (but which are actually designed to improve your typing and keyboard skills). Mavis will even remind you to take a break or sit up straight! Conveniently, the software contains 25 minutes of video footage demonstrating the safest and most comfortable keyboard habits.

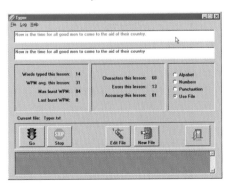

The interface for Typor Typing Tutor *is simplicity itself. Copy the practice sentence – and check your mistakes in green text in the bottom window.*

● Inexpensive options

Shareware offers a host of typing tutors. A good example is *Typor Typing Tutor*, which displays the text to be copied in one box and your keystrokes in another. Only correct keystrokes go into the box, but all keystrokes are displayed in green in the window below. This way you can see at a glance the keys with which you are having trouble. The program monitors the number of words typed, the number of errors and the average words typed per minute.

● Young typists

Animated Beginning Typing for Windows is designed for young typists and teaches proper typing technique for the letter keys. Sound effects and animation are used to

make learning fun and to keep your attention sharp as you learn. Help is provided through the animated tutorial, a screen to show proper fingering and an on-screen keyboard which highlights the correct key when needed.

Learning to type on a *professional level rather than just acquiring basic keyboard skills is a long process, taking many weeks. Top-of-the-range tutors like* Mavis Beacon *provide a carefully structured course that will take you right through to an advanced level. They even provide diversions in the form of games, which allow you to have fun while practicing essential typing techniques.*

CONTACT POINTS

Mavis Beacon Teaches Typing
Broderbund
Tel: 1 800 395 0277
Price: $19.95

Shareware
A catalogue of shareware titles can be found at such sites as:
http://download.cnet.com
or
www.tucows.com

At the movies

Lights! Camera! Action! Bring all the adventure and romance of the movies into your home, straight from the silver screen onto your computer screen.

The connection between your PC and the movies can be traced back to the very first few games that were written for the earliest home computers.

A *Star Trek* game was released even before the first *Star Trek* feature film was made. Based on the TV series, it was one of the first examples of a computer game picking up on popular culture. However, with its tiny '*' character representing the spaceship, it could not look more basic compared with today's CD-ROM multimedia spectaculars.

● Hollywood and video games
After many years of video games based on movies, there are now movies based on video games. Unfortunately, films such as *Super*

Mario Bros, Mortal Kombat 1 & 2 and *Wing Commander* all proved to be pretty poor, and critics panned the *Tomb Raider* movie – featuring a 'real' Lara Croft, played by Angelina Jolie. We still await the much-delayed film version of shoot-'em-ups such as *Doom* and *Quake*.

Indiana Jones and the Infernal Machine *marks Dr. Jones' fifth outing on the PC, but his first in 3D.*

● The right connections
Your PC has movie connections in more ways than just game playing, though: there are interactive film guides available on CD-ROM; you'll find movie websites run by both the film companies and devoted fans; and powerful computers have been used by movie studios to create entire films, with only the voices being provided by real actors and actresses.

● Essential merchandise
When a film has been released, a spin-off game can become a major part of the merchandising throughout the shelf life of the film. Even if the film had nothing whatsoever to do with computers or the Internet, by the time it is released it will almost certainly have taken up a place in one of the increasing number of PC movie guides.

● Games based on films
The science fiction genre, of course, seems to lend itself to the medium of computer games particularly well, but you will also find other types of film on your PC. After the video game version of *Indiana Jones and the Last Crusade* came a new graphic adventure, *Indiana Jones and the Fate of the Atlantis*, with a completely original plot. The game was so good that it's rumored to be the basis of the fourth *Indiana Jones* film. Even if that film doesn't get made, there is now a new 3D *Indiana Jones* game on its way as well.

Other film series have struggled to produce games that do them justice. Although several attempts have been made over the years, there has never been a truly satisfying game based on the *Jurassic Park* or *James Bond* films.

HOW MOVIES INFLUENCE GAMES

For every game that is officially licensed from a motion picture, there are a dozen unofficially 'influenced' ones. In fact, there is scarcely a science fiction game in existence that hasn't been influenced by classic films such as *Star Wars*, *Alien* and *The Terminator*. Other types of film have also influenced some recent titles. *Resident Evil* seems to owe most of its plot to George Romero's series of zombie movies, and the classic *Driver* game appears to be based on the car chases in the Steve McQueen film *Bullitt*, even down to the San Francisco setting and cars used.

In part, this seems to be because some films, no matter how action-oriented they may be, just don't translate well to the PC screen; even the longest of films tends to have only three or four unique action scenes and this just isn't enough to fill even the shallowest of PC games.

The most successful movie-based games are those set within the 'universe' of a film, but which aren't strictly based on the movie's plot. The original *Star Trek* games, which have the freedom to create a plot better suited to a computer game, always tend to be more successful than those trying to translate a two-hour film script into a game with more than 40 hours of gameplay. The *Star Trek* game, *Generations*, is a great example that takes full advantage of your PC's multimedia abilities.

Film itself may be on the way out. Some films – such as Disney's Toy Story – have been made almost entirely on large banks of powerful computers.

May the force be with you!

LUCASARTS RELEASED their behind-the-scenes guide to the world of *Star Wars* just as the hype for the 'prequel' *Episode I – The Phantom Menace* was beginning to build up. *Behind the Magic* is the best example of many similar movie guides, excelling through its superb presentation and attention to detail. Care has been taken to make sure that those with only a passing interest in the films can still find something to amuse them. In fact, the guide has often been described as more fun to use than some games are to play.

Behind the Magic features a plethora of previously unseen material. This includes interviews with cast and crew, video footage of some hilariously bad auditions from the original cast, and a number of scenes cut from the first film that can be seen only as a part of this package.

Characters

This section contains information on a huge range of characters from the *Star Wars* movies, novels and comics. It is split into three sections: Main Characters; Aliens & Creatures; Groups & Organizations. Depending on their prominence within the movies, each entry may have a full biography, image gallery, video and sound clips, behind-the-scenes information and even a trivia question.

Technology

The Technology section looks at the vehicles, weapons and devices of the *Star Wars* universe. Each item has its own screen of information organized in a similar manner to the Character entries, although here each ship has its own rotatable 3D model for you to examine. Highlights of this section include a 3D walking tour of the Millennium Falcon and an interactive 'weapons test'.

Use your PC to delve into the amazing world of *Star Wars*.

Episode 1 preview

This sneak peek at the most recent *Star Wars* movie doesn't reveal much in the way of plot details or images, but is an interesting taster of the movie, with detailed pictures and models and some fascinating interviews.

Scene by scene

Perhaps the most interesting section of the guide includes an annotated scene-by-scene script guide, complete with production notes, images and commentary from George Lucas and many of his crew members.

From film reels to CD-ROM

There have been film licenses since the earliest days of video gaming. Here are some of the more recent offerings.

IN THE EARLY DAYS of video games, film licenses had a poor reputation. Often the license was added at a late stage in a title's development, simply to bolster the appeal of an otherwise lackluster product.

Nowadays game makers are more in tune with the movies, although many titles do still fall into the trap of featuring too many game styles in a vain attempt to simulate every action scene in a film. Over the next two pages we'll look at some classic examples of movie-licensed games. Most of them are successful games in their own right and, rather than being afterthoughts, are produced with help from the original movie crew and actors.

Star Wars: Episode I – The Phantom Menace

As if there weren't enough *Star Wars* games already, George Lucas' own company LucasArts has released a game based on the new 'prequel' – the first of the new trilogy of films. The game is a departure from previous *Star Wars* games in that for the first time it attempts to follow the entire plot of one of the films. Most of the game is played from an innovative quasi-overhead viewpoint. Players can take control of four of the film's main characters: Obi-Wan Kenobi, Qui-Gon Jinn, Queen Amidala and Captain Panaka.

The game's publishers planned for this title to be one of the biggest selling video games ever, thanks to a high-profile simultaneous launch on both the PC and the PlayStation games console.

Blade Runner

Science fiction films and computer games go together like bacon and eggs. But there's a world of difference between the action-based *Star Wars* movies and the more cerebral style of *Blade Runner*. Not a big hit on its original release, the film has since achieved a cult following and is widely regarded as one of the best 'serious' science fiction films ever made. Fittingly, the game is far from being a simple shoot-'em-up, but is instead a dialogue-

oriented graphic adventure. To make sure that the plot is not predictable, the game's story is different from the film's, although most of the central characters look and act similarly to those that Harrison Ford encountered. Although the game comes across as a watered-down version of the film, it is a brave and rare attempt at an intelligent adult adventure.

Braveheart

Braveheart is a rather unusual film to find being converted to game form, for like the film games of old, the license to Mel Gibson's epic was only added late in the game's development. Fittingly produced by a Scottish programming team, *Braveheart* is a real-time strategy game that has you controlling the fate of the Scottish nation in an attempt to unite the various clans and defeat the invading English.

The game is split between two basic tasks: fighting various 3D battles across Scotland, and controlling the overall political picture via various overhead maps and status screens.

Trespasser

The two *Jurassic Park* films have yet to spawn a truly successful video game. Although the movies are essentially action films, the most important set pieces usually involve little human interaction with the dinosaurs, which makes a more literal game translation difficult.

The latest gaming attempt, *Trespasser*, is actually a sequel to *The Lost World* and sees an intrepid female character stranded on a dinosaur-filled island.

WarGames

Games don't always have to be based on the latest cinema hit. *WarGames* was a hit film from the 1980s which portrayed the story of a high-school computer hacker breaking into a US nuclear defense computer. The game is a real-time strategy in the style of *Command & Conquer*, albeit with some impressive 3D graphics – a first for the genre. The premise is that you are the hacker trying to win a virtual war game against a computer to prevent it starting a real war.

A Bug's Life Action Game

Disney Interactive's action game, derived from the computer-animated movie *A Bug's Life*, is from the old style of licensed video games. It follows the plot of the film fairly rigidly and the game style is an obvious variant on a popular style of the day – in this case the celebrated *Tomb Raider* series of 3D platform games. Clearly aimed at a younger audience, the game is competently put together, but makes little attempt at originality or furthering its particular genre.

Aliens vs. Predator

There has, as yet, been no such movie as *Aliens vs. Predator*. But the idea of these two modern-day movie monsters fighting it out has long ago been explored in a series of well-regarded comic books, from which an unfilmed movie script was derived. However, where cinema fears to tread, video games rush in, and this is only the latest – and by far the most successful – of various attempts to make a game from the concept. *Aliens vs. Predator* is essentially a *Quake*-style 3D shoot-'em-up with the twist that you can take the role of either a monster or a luckless human marine. The game is excellent at portraying all the protagonists.

Top Gun: Hornet's Nest

No matter how old some films are, they are always viewed as ripe subject matter for video games. As with many popular action films, *Top Gun* has appeared in various pixelized forms over the years. The 1995 hit *Top Gun: Fire at Will*! was an imaginative mix of hard-core flight simulator and more arcade-style action, complete with a well-acted storyline featuring some actors from the original film. *Hornet's Nest*, however, is a more dumbed-down approach to the same idea with the emphasis firmly on flight simulation. But it still features James Tolkan as Hondo, and helps to prove that some movies, and their games, never die.

The world on a disc

With a CD-ROM atlas you can experience sights and sounds from anywhere in the world – without ever leaving the comfort of your own home.

Microsoft's Encarta Interactive World Atlas 2001 is more than just a reference guide to the countries of the world: it also explains the facts behind the Earth's makeup.

Audio and visual clips help to give you a better insight into the diverse nature of the planet and the different peoples of the world.

There are few books as interesting or as instructive as a good atlas, with its combination of detailed maps, fascinating statistics and explanations of how the Earth has developed since its origins. But can the CD-ROM atlas outdo its printed counterpart in terms of presentation and detail?

In many respects it can, through the addition of elements, such as video, photographs and sound, together with the use of dynamic links between different types of information. In a printed atlas, you would have to look at a map page, find the relevant statistical page,

then turn to yet another section to find out about the physical geography of the area you are considering. Yet, with a CD-ROM atlas, a few clicks of the mouse will bring up all that data on your screen as the questions present themselves – and also throw in a video clip with narration or music for good measure. As a result, you can learn the broadest aspects of geography in a way that often feels more natural than using a book.

● The world at your fingertips

The Microsoft *Encarta Interactive World Atlas 2001* demonstrates this well. The core information itself is first class and the maps are clear and attractive, letting you zoom in close to see a greater amount of detail. The double CD-ROM set also lets you zoom out to satellite views to get the bigger picture. A variety of map styles is available and the depth of the

Incredible 3D virtual flights allow you to look at the world in which we live from every conceivable angle – from city maps at street level, to views from space.

CONTACT POINTS

My First Amazing World Explorer
Price $19.99

Eyewitness World Atlas
Price $49.95
Dorling Kindersley Multimedia
Tel: 1 212 213 4800

Encarta Interactive World Atlas 2001
Microsoft
Tel: 1 888 218 5617
Price $34.95

Dorling Kindersley's My First Amazing World Explorer is far more than just an atlas on CD-ROM. Incorporating books, stickers, a poster and picture postcards, this activity pack will take your child on a fun-packed learning adventure.

accompanying information is equally impressive.

Country articles give you not only the geography, but also the history, language and customs, accompanied by a rich variety of photographs. Also, nearly everywhere on the globe has an associated sound clip featuring typical music of the region. The multimedia angle is rounded off with a feature that is by no means essential, but is certainly a lot of fun, and that is the Virtual Flight.

● Where shall we go today?

Floating through the Grand Canyon or the Alps to the accompaniment of a suitably dreamy soundtrack might not do much to improve a school geography grade, but it will certainly be a pleasure that could tempt you back to the software and its other attractive features.

Dorling Kindersley's *Eyewitness World Atlas* is likewise strong on reference material, although it does not have quite so many multimedia features as *Encarta*. It is presented as a hybrid atlas/encyclopedia/gazetteer, and it relies as much on statistical information as on its maps.

The *Interactive World Atlas* from Focus Multimedia lacks some of the finesse of the Microsoft and Dorling Kindersley atlases, but is nevertheless a useful and informative disc. The large-scale maps are not particularly attractive, but they improve when you zoom in. You can then click on the signposts dotted around to get detailed local information, such as the area of a lake in Sweden.

Become A World Explorer, from Dorling Kindersley is not really an atlas but it has enough factual knowledge to keep any four-to-nine-year-old interested. It contains a CD-ROM, an activity book, a jigsaw puzzle, a poster and some postcards. The CD-ROM starts with a soundtrack of instruments, such as the didgeridoo and the zither, and takes you into a child's bedroom – the beginning of a round of geographic adventures that take you off on 19 journeys around the globe, entitling you to a World Explorer Certificate.

World wise

Dorling Kindersley's Eyewitness World Atlas is a comprehensive world guide.

Know the global facts

Detailed charts and graphs help to provide an in-depth examination of every country in the world. You can also compare statistics between one nation and another.

Helping to put you in the picture

Photographs and videos of more than 250 of the world's most dramatic cities and landscapes help to bring faraway places to life.

Find your way around the planet

Simple navigational tools allow you access to high quality maps and background information on every nation in the world.

Games for all

Are PC games all as violent and unsuitable for children as they are made out to be? The simple answer is 'No'. Choose your games carefully and they will provide education and entertainment for all the family.

I t was not long ago that many people were transfixed by the sight of a simple white dot as they batted it from one side of the screen to the other. Today, however, this classic tennis game, called *Pong*, would keep the average game-player's attention for only a relatively short time.

Computer games have developed quickly from simple exercises to multimedia experiences that seem to have more in common with television or the movies. Today's multimedia PCs can have CD-quality stereo sound and a monitor that can display millions of colors to satisfy your ears and eyes, while the keys on the keyboard and the mouse will keep your hands busy. The program creator can put many different elements into a game, and there are thousands of games available.

● Choose carefully

Just as a video store contains films that are suitable only for informed adults, the range of computer game titles includes many that are inappropriate for family use. Parents should use the same judgment on the suitability of a computer game as they would on a rented video. One of the best ways to do this is to check the game packaging for information about the age group at which the game is aimed. Reading reviews of games also gives a good indication of whether they are actually suitable for the whole family to use.

You can also look for games that have parental control settings. These contain versions for adults and children. When the game is loaded, parents can set a secret password that prevents children accessing the adult aspects of the game, but still allows children to enjoy a perfectly playable version.

● Check points

The number, range and content of games are extremely confusing. Many

Games such as SimCity 3000, Age of Empires, Rollercoaster Tycoon and Star Trek are not only fun for all the family, but in their own way, can be an educational experience as well.

BEFORE YOU BUY

When buying a game, look on the box for the suitable age indicator that warns parents of the potential violent content of a game. This usually shows the age range that the game was designed for, such as 3–10, 7–11, 11–14 or 18+.

people select games on the recommendation of friends or work colleagues, but what if you want to choose something new? The first point to consider is who the game is for. If it is solely for you, then you can choose a title that you find interesting personally. If it is for other members of your family as well, you may want to choose a game with wider appeal. Then you need to be sure that the game will work on your computer. Look carefully at the minimum PC requirements printed on the packaging. Also, be aware that games can come on a CD-ROM or 3.5 inch disk (although floppy disks are becoming increasingly rare).

Another point to bear in mind is what the game is for. Many games are purely for the player's enjoyment. Others have a strong educational content – some specifically for children to help them practice the topics they are learning at school and some designed for adults who may want to explore a new area of learning. Some of the best family games successfully combine entertainment with education.

● Games to suit every taste

When you look at the range of games stacked on the shelves of software stores and PC superstores, you soon realize that there is a title to suit most tastes and age groups. Choosing one to entertain you can be baffling, even if you have a general idea of the type of game you want.

One of the largest groups of games is strategy, or mind games (see pages

126–127). Mainly aimed at adults, these are games that you could easily find occupying a whole weekend. The best strategy games present you with a scenario in which you have to survive and thrive. A good example is *Civilization: Call To Power*, which casts you as the leader of a tribe. By making political, military, diplomatic, technological and economic decisions, your goal is to improve the fortunes and power of your people. Every decision you make has repercussions with which you will have to live in the future. The aim is to become the dominant people on Earth.

● An awfully big adventure

Adventure gaming is one of the oldest genres, dating back to the earliest mainframe computers. This type of game is played out in a large number of beautifully drawn locations. Depending on the plot, these can be anything from a bleak cityscape to a tongue-in-cheek Caribbean pirate island. Or, in the case of the popular *Grim Fandango*, a bizarre representation of the land of the dead as a 1930s-influenced art deco world.

Unlike other game styles, lateral thinking is the prime requisite for adventure games. Controlling your

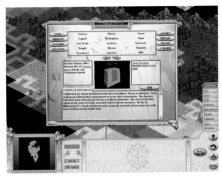

Lead your civilization to world supremacy by manipulating destiny from the Stone Age to the year 3000 A.D. **Call To Power** *contains detailed information on a huge range of historical technologies, concepts and events.*

on-screen character, you must travel from place to place, as the storyline and your quest within it demands, seeking clues and meeting various helpful, knowledgeable or unsavory characters. Interacting with these characters plays an equal part with the manipulation of items in your inventory, as you use anything and everything in your possession to reach your goal.

The other prerequisite for the majority of adventure games is a sense of humor. Unlike many other games, humor plays a big part in most adventure titles and can be surprisingly subtle and clever. Some games, such as the long-running

Combine a good game with the Internet and you get a great game. With Monster Truck Madness 2, you log on to a special Internet site, choose your vehicle and race against players around the world.

LONG PLAY?

There is a great debate about whether computer games are bad for children, and as with many arguments the answer lies somewhere between two opposing points of view. Of course, every case is different, but, generally, moderate game playing can be instructive, particularly if the game is educational. Children can learn from the content of the game, and, just from the act of playing, will even improve their keyboard and mouse skills. They might also learn more about how the computer works.

CHECKPOINT ✔

WORK ON MY PC?

Check on the packaging to make sure the game is compatible with your computer, and that the PC has enough memory to play it. This information will usually be under the heading 'Minimum Requirements'. This gives details of the following requirements of a game:

☑ the type and speed of computer processor (Pentium, Pentium II, III and 4)
☑ minimum memory requirements (RAM)
☑ number of on-screen colors
☑ sound card
☑ operating system (Windows 95, 98, Me, and XP)
☑ 3D graphics accelerator
☑ the type of input devices supported – mouse, joystick or keyboard – and whether they are a requirement.

If you're unsure of the specifications of your PC, look in its manual or contact the store you bought it from. Take the details with you when you buy.

Monkey Island series, are full-blown comedies with a more mature and original sense of humor than you'll see in most feature films.

Sports games have always been popular activities on the PC. Perhaps they give the player a chance at athletic glory that they wouldn't otherwise have. Very few sports have been ignored by the computer games makers. You can play everything from football, golf and pool to Formula 1 racing.

Some games are more successful in their transfer to the PC than others. Golf and pool work well, but team games such as football and ice hockey are a little trickier to master. Some strive hard to

If it's raining outside, you can sit down and play golf with Arnold Palmer on a recreation of the famous Old Course at St. Andrews in Scotland. With wet grass and fog as options, Links LS 2000 *is very realistic.*

achieve high levels of realism. In *Colin McRae Rally*, for example, you can tweak almost every aspect of your car's setup to shave crucial tenths of a second off your time.

One of the best aspects of sports games for families is that, in many of them, two or more people can play at the same time. In a game such as golf, you can even have your own family tournament.

There are PC games available for all ages, including the very young. Now even the preschooler can enjoy an interactive story or simple adventure with an educational element, such as those you will find on the CD-ROMs made by *JumpStart*. Some of these award-winning programs help toddlers leap to an early understanding of learning activities, teaching them to chase letters, sort objects, and understand prepositions. For example, in the *JumpStart Preschool Deluxe*, suitable for children from 2-5 years, there are 11 modules, each with three levels of difficulty, covering over 40 educational areas including reading readiness, memory development, numeral recognition and auditory discrimination.

● Plane speaking

If you dream of heading off into the wild blue yonder, flight simulators are ideal for taking to the skies while keeping your feet firmly on the ground. You can fly a large airliner

Humongous Entertainment specializes in children's games such as the Putt-Putt series. In the game shown here, Putt-Putt joins the circus.

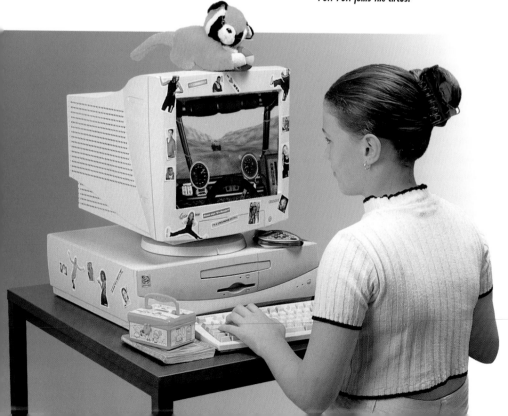

across America, practice your taking off and landing techniques in a Cessna 152, or streak across the skies at twice the speed of sound in the latest stealth fighter.

Programs such as Microsoft *Flight Simulator* and Eidos' *Flight Unlimited* series or *Fly! II* are unmatched for realism and detail – so much so that real pilots and trainees use them to practice their skills. If you crave a bit more

excitement, then you might prefer to go for a combat flight simulator. These are just as detailed – one company making combat flight simulations also produces software for real fighter pilots – and allow you to take part in complex missions simulating aspects of modern aerial warfare. It's pretty tricky to fly a plane and shoot things at the same time, but that's the challenge.

● Action heroes

There are also a huge number and variety of nonstop action games. In many, the focus is on fighting and shooting, but there are others that are more suitable for children.

An action game doesn't have to be gory, and titles such as *Croc* feature gameplay similar to that of *Tomb Raider*, but with graphics and features aimed squarely at the preteen market. Jumping across platforms and rescuing friendly animals is the order of the day, rather than fighting off disgusting intergalactic mutants.

The most popular type of action game is the 'first-person shoot-'em-up'. Viewing a 3D landscape, basically 'if it moves, you shoot it'. You run, jump, shoot and swim your way around detailed mazes, tunnels and buildings. The *Quake* series, *Unreal* and *Half-Life*, are the most popular 3D action games.

Guide Lara Croft around the huge 3D environments in the blockbusting Tomb Raider *series. Lara is the world's first computer-generated sex symbol, but the game requires a lot more strategic thought than you would first imagine.*

If you don't want to be responsible for a whole country, how about a soccer team? Championship Manager 3 *is one of the best-selling PC games. It goes into incredible detail about field tactics and the abilities of your players.*

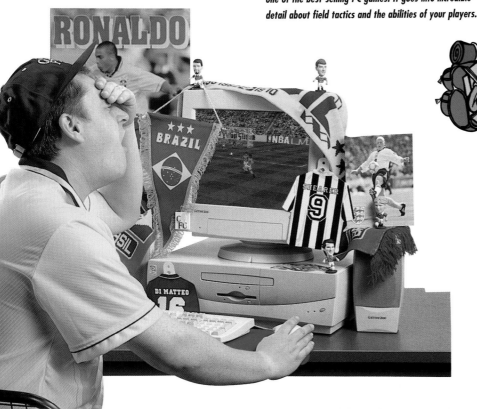

Kicking off with soccer games

Simple objectives, fast action and an infinite number of subtleties and strategies make soccer one of the best examples of the computer sports game.

With an official license, FIFA soccer games include the world's biggest club teams as well as the international teams.

As soon as programmers could make graphics move around a screen, they tried to reproduce soccer playing on a computer. And it's easy to see why; soccer is the most popular spectator sport in the world; it's fast, simple to understand and has a vast number of subtleties. Early PC versions of the game had only a passing resemblance to the real thing: one of the earliest, *International Soccer*, had only one player on each team (plus a goalie) and an almost two-dimensional playing field. Today, soccer games not only have whole teams, but 'motion-capture' from top players and the vocal talents of well-known international sports commentators.

● Serious about soccer

The *FIFA* soccer series, published by Electronic Arts, is the most commercially successful soccer game in the world, and it's also one of the most accurate renditions of the game available. It is updated once a year and is generally identified as simply *FIFA 99*, *FIFA 2001* and so on. It has always been a huge seller, thanks to an official license that grants the use of players' real names and faces.

Before starting a match, you choose your team. The value of the official license really shows in the depth of choice available. In addition to teams from our own Major League Soccer (MLS), you can choose teams from leagues in more than a dozen foreign leagues, including Brazil, England and Italy.

The International choice is just as diverse, with over 40 of the world's top teams – USA included – to choose from. Once you've chosen the two teams, you get to decide on other variables such as the stadium, field type, weather conditions and so on. You also select how long you wish to play a match for. Five or 10 minutes is a common option.

When the game starts you see a portion of the field from an angle similar to that used in TV coverage and you are in control of the player closest to the ball. In theory you have control over the whole team, but in practice you control only one player, and unless you choose otherwise it is always the player nearest to the ball. You move him around the field using the directional controls on a joystick or keypad and use a number of other buttons to kick, pass, run and shoot.

● The competition

The gameplay and depth of graphics in Microsoft's *International Soccer 2000* is broadly similar to the FIFA series. Like Electronic Arts, Microsoft has studied motion capture footage of real players to improve realism – over 9,000 frames covering 200 individual moves.

SOCCER MANAGEMENT

If you find yourself as fascinated by soccer management as you are by playing tactics, you can try the role of a manager of a team. There are on-line versions of the *Fantasy Soccer* games run by overseas newspapers: you manage the finances of the club, buying and selling players with the overall aim of winning the championship. There's often a substantial cash prize at stake, too. To get a feel for these games visit one of the popular sites for England's soccer Premier League www.telegraph premierleague.com, or use a search engine to findon-line fantasy soccer leagues elsewhere in the world. Don't forget, though: soccer is known as football in most of the rest of the world.

Microsoft may lack the FIFA license, but its International Soccer 2000 game still allows you to play club and international games.

The graphics in the FIFA games, by Electronic Arts, are the best of their kind, capturing the stadium atmosphere perfectly.

To make the gameplay easy for novices to get into, Microsoft has adopted a one-touch control system that helps you to get started. This is useful because it helps to prevent the frustrating experience of finding that your computer-controlled opposition is winning easily as you try to get a grip on player movement and actions.

● Family fun

Soccer is one of the fastest growing sports for kids – thanks largely to the fact that it needs no extra equipment beyond a ball and something to mark a goal. The success of the U.S. Women's National Team in international competition has also made soccer a lot more popular among girls in the U.S. than in the rest of the world.

Reflecting both aspects, Humongous Entertainment has developed *Backyard Soccer MLS Edition*, an altogether more kid-friendly way into computerized soccer. The neat twist in this game is that famous players from the MLS (such as Los Angeles Galaxy's Cobi Jones) and the U.S. Women's National Team (such as Brandi Chastain) appear as kids for you to select for your team. Letting your kids rub virtual shoulders with such major stars is a great motivational boost.

Gameplay is very different than with adult-oriented soccer games like *FIFA 2001*. You need to be pretty accurate with the mouse,

clicking on the player you want to move and then the position you want to move him to. The simplicity of the game reflects the age group it's aimed at: 5-10 year-olds who would find the range of skills needed to master *FIFA* games off-putting.

● Learning soccer skills

If you prefer real soccer to virtual soccer, you can use your PC to get help with your training. *Brazilian Soccer Skills and Tactics* with Zico is a 2 CD-ROM pack that uses interactive video to help impart Zico's legendary ball skills. *Tactics 4.0* is a much more serious affair – created originally to help Italian soccer managers plan tactics and specific plays. Both are available from www.soccerevolution.com.

Backyard Soccer makes the most of the US Women's Soccer Team success in World Cup football, pitching this kid-friendly game at girls as well as boys.

Representing world famous players – such as the Colorado Rapids' Carlos Valderama – as kids, is a novel twist that adds to the appeal of Backyard Soccer.

CONTACT POINTS

There is a huge range of soccer games available, particularly when a big tournament is taking place. The following titles, though, have proven to be popular through the years. Many are updated on a regular basis to take account both of new player signings to teams in the world of real soccer and advances in the exciting virtual world of computer graphics technology.

FIFA 2001
Price: $39.95
Electronic Arts (EA Sports)
Tel: 1 877 324 2637

Backyard Soccer
Price: $30
Humongous Entertainment
www.humongous.com/

International Soccer
Price: $19.95
Microsoft
Tel: 1 888 218 5617

Mind games

The qualities that make board games, such as chess and backgammon, so enduringly popular have been successfully transferred to mind – or strategy – games on the computer. To overcome the challenge of your opponent, be it another player or the PC itself, you need skill, planning and good powers of concentration.

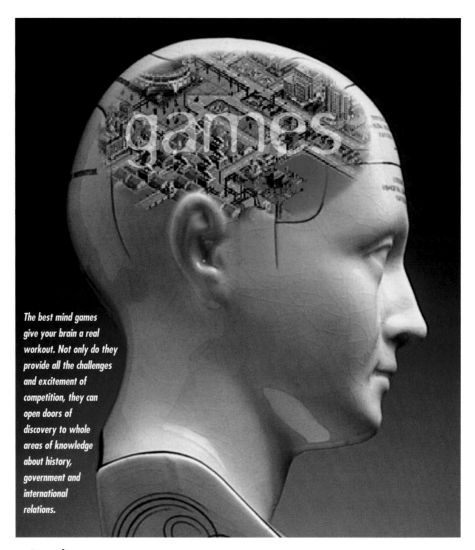

The best mind games give your brain a real workout. Not only do they provide all the challenges and excitement of competition, they can open doors of discovery to whole areas of knowledge about history, government and international relations.

Mind games have been played on computers ever since the first programmers created ticktacktoe and chess games. Today's top chess programs can beat Grand Masters, but less daunting mind games are available for the rest of us. They don't involve any of the violence that is found in the shooting and fighting games, there are no car chases, explosions or aircraft dogfights, but they can be just as exciting.

● **Play the classics**
Apart from classic games such as chess and backgammon, there are now more and more commercial games, including the family favorites *Monopoly*, *Risk* and *Clue*, being converted for you to play on your home computer.

For a different challenge, you can tackle one of the many puzzle games developed for people with leisure time to spend in front of their PC.

● **Beat the computer**
Computer mind games aren't so much about beating an opponent, but defeating your powerful computer. And beware – these games can be incredibly absorbing. You may intend to play for just 20 minutes, but find that several hours have elapsed by the time you finally concede defeat or triumph over your PC.

● **A simple challenge**
With many of the most popular games, the task you have to perform successfully is often deceptively simple. In *Tetris*, for example, you must guide the colored shapes as they drop down the screen, so that when they reach the bottom they lock together and form complete lines. The more you concentrate on which shapes are coming next, the longer you will be able to play, and the higher your score will be. The instant appeal of the game comes from its colorful simplicity. With hardly any

rules and easy controls, it's the ideal game for first-time computer users. They will be able to start playing right away, and while they are concentrating on moving the shapes effectively, their fingers will be

Variants of the classic Tetris game have been around for years – the latest is The Next Tetris. The basic gameplay remains the same: geometric shapes fall from the top of the screen and need to be arranged so that they connect together at the bottom and form a solid line.

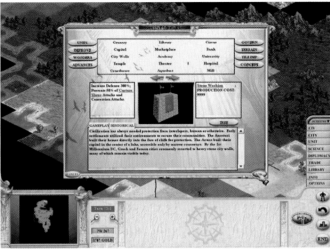

making themselves at home on the previously unfamiliar PC keyboard.

● The good soldier

For a greater challenge, there are global strategy games. The board-based forerunner of this game type was *Risk*, where players tried to conquer the world by military means alone and success or failure rested on the roll of the dice. Much more than luck is needed if you are to succeed in the latest global strategy games.

Play the baddie for a change in Dungeon Keeper 2. Build your own dungeon, keep the monsters on your side and set traps in case a hero comes after your gold.

A popular one is *Civilization: Call To Power*, in which you begin as the leader of a primitive tribe and you must guide it in a quest to dominate the world and conquer space. You help your people to explore the world, build armies, defeat rival civilizations and form strategic alliances with other powerful nations. You can also research new leaps in technology, starting with basics, such as the wheel or an alphabet. Then you graduate to choosing a form of government, such as a

Assess your leadership potential with Civilization: Call To Power. You have to guide your tribe from the Stone Age to the space age using skill, courage and ingenuity.

republic or monarchy, and you move on to mass production, recycling and even space travel.

To be successful at the game, the decisions you make must be wise ones based on all the knowledge you have accumulated – the game does not work on just a random basis. This type of strategy game is a great way to encourage reluctant young students to start learning about what makes society tick.

● Dig out the dungeon

Dungeon Keeper 2 is a game that lets you see how the other half lives. Instead of you being the good conquering evil, you become the evil keeper of a dungeon. You and your servant imps dig out rooms to create monster lairs, training rooms and food stores. Unfortunately, these attract giant beetles, warlocks and demons to your dungeon. Add a workshop and library and you can create a fighting force armed with spells and traps. Improve and expand your dungeon into the surrounding area, and trolls and dragons may join your ranks. You'll need these on your side as the local heroes soon come calling at your dungeon door.

● Pleasing the people

A little closer to us mortals is the role of city mayor in the game called *SimCity 3000*. You still get to wield

power and decide how to build your ultimate city, but now you have to use political cunning and tact because there are voters to please.

If you take too many liberties, you'll be thrown out of office. So, if you don't plan carefully while your city expands with a mix of residential, commercial and industrial areas, and you set an excessive tax rate, your voters will refuse to cooperate. Instead, they'll complain about crime, pollution and overcrowded roads.

The Internet

Introducing the Internet

The Internet lets you travel around the globe at the click of your mouse. Step onto the information superhighway and discover how your PC can give you a window looking out over the whole world.

There is something on the Internet for everybody – not just businessmen and academics. From your home, you can connect to millions of other computers all over the world and find information about almost any subject you want.

and much more. You'll find text, sound, pictures and even video clips. You can subscribe to discussion groups and participate in discussions with thousands of like-minded people around the world. Many of these groups have specific interests, with well over 10,000 different topics covered.

● Email for free
Email (or electronic mail) is the fastest way to communicate with the millions of other users on the Internet. You can send letters and files from your PC without the cost of a stamp, and it's almost instantaneous – you can often receive a reply from the other side of the world within minutes.

● Just browsing
The World Wide Web is the name of the network of links that connects all the different Internet sites. It is probably the most popular part of the Net. With a browser, you can use the World Wide Web to access information on the Internet.

The Internet is a worldwide network of computers linked together by high-speed cables. There are millions of computers making up this information superhighway – some the size of a small building, others the same size and type as your home PC. This means that anyone with a PC and a modem can become part of the Internet by connecting through an ordinary telephone line.

Once you're connected, the real power and interest of the Internet becomes apparent. This huge network of computers is as easy to use as your own PC. Just as you click your way around the programs and files on your computer with Windows, the Internet lets you click your way around this worldwide information network.

● Something for everyone
There are computers (or Internet sites) that cover every subject imaginable: celebrities and entertainment, sports, news, science

INTERNET ORIGINS

Although it has only recently been available to the general public, the Internet has existed since the late 1960s. It was originally designed by the US military as a way of protecting its main computer facilities in the event of a nuclear attack. With the advent of the World Wide Web in 1989, the Internet became so flexible that almost anyone in the world could connect his or her computer to the system.

Exploring the World Wide Web

The Web is huge – hundreds of thousands of places to visit and every interest under the sun provided for. It's as diverse as the world itself.

INFORMATION on anything you care to name is available on the World Wide Web. To help you find it, easy-to-use Web searching tools will locate the sites covering subjects you're interested in. The search tools are not programs that you need to buy and install on your computer, they are special websites themselves. Once your computer is set up with a modem, plugged into the telephone line and you have selected an Internet service provider (we'll explain what this is on pages 136–137), you can log on whenever you wish.

Websites are made up of interactive pages; you click on a link and something happens – you might jump to a new page, start a video clip or hear a sound recording.

Instead of starting on page one and reading to the end, as you do with most books, with a website you jump back and forward as your interest takes you. Many sites don't look like book pages at all; some have amazing 3D worlds to explore. Here are some of the types of websites you will be able to browse when your PC is on the information superhighway.

SHOPPING

This site for JCPenney, the catalog and department store retailer – http://www.jcpenney.com – is a typical online store. You can view the catalog and place your order online. Simply click on the items you want, review the final details on the order form, then another mouse click instantly sends your order.

Click here to check what special offers are available in the sale.

THE Internet is becoming the largest superstore. You can visit your favorite store or browse through online shopping centers, which bring together stores selling a wide range of goods and services. JCPenney.com and Sears.com are just two of the most popular sites.

You can order almost anything from the thousands of online shops, using your credit card. It will then be delivered to your home.

NEWS

OFFERING unparalleled access to world news and current affairs, the Internet lets you keep up with the latest stories as they happen.

Newspapers from around the world are available online, and TV news services, such as CNN and Sky TV, also offer excellent coverage.

There are even special interest news sites, including some designed especially for children.

News from all over the world can be picked up almost as soon as it happens. The CNN site – http://cnn.com – divides all news into key categories, such as US news, world news, world weather and so on. This is the Nature page, which deals with environmental issues.

This link takes you to the story behind the headline in full. Or, if you want to see a larger version of the picture, just click on it.

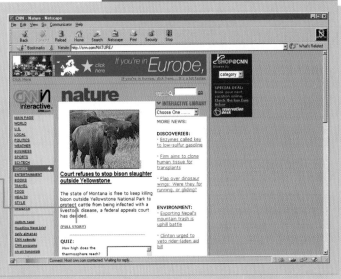

WHATEVER your favorite sport, it is likely to have at least one devoted fan who has prepared a website dedicated to it. By visiting the site, you can pick up the latest news and gossip, and chat to other fans around the world.

As you might expect, soccer fans are well provided for on the Web with a mass of information on famous teams, league positions, games and player profiles.

A racing fan can go straight to the official Ferrari site – http://www.ferrari.it – and get the inside track on the team. One of the best things about sports sites is that they are updated frequently.

Pick your favorite Ferrari – this link lists every model made, with pictures, technical specifications and performance details.

This link will take you to the page where future races and Ferrari developments are detailed.

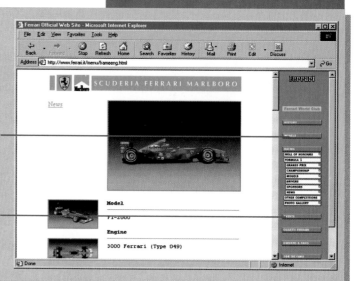

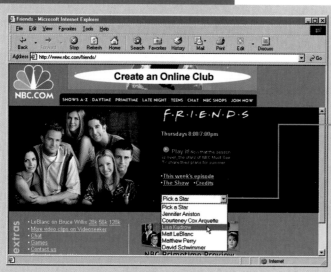

A very popular site is that of the television show *Friends* – http://www.nbc.com/friends. Here you can discover everything you wanted to know about the show and its stars.

Select a name here to go to your favorite character's own pages, where there are pictures and stories about them. Read about shows you missed, find out who does what behind the scenes and download (transfer) pictures onto your computer.

KEEPING up with your favorite band, finding out about exhibitions or simply organizing your TV viewing is easy on the Web. Major TV companies have their own sites where you can find a wealth of information on TV shows and the antics of your favorite celebrities.

If you want to locate a restaurant, see a movie, or read about an interesting new bar, you will find the Internet a great resource.

YOU can study for school or college and even obtain a degree using the Internet. Universities from around the world have sites and some offer online courses.

Most schools now have an Internet connection, and many schoolchildren use it for research and to keep in touch with a penpal abroad. Children can also visit special online exhibitions created by world-famous museums.

Whatever the homework assignment, there's a museum or education site to help out. Here, the University of California Museum – http://www.ucmp.berkeley.edu/ – has a new dinosaur exhibition.

Here's a link that will tell you about more dinosaurs and lead you to other dinosaur sites.

Click here for more detailed information about the *Tyrannosaurus rex* in the picture.

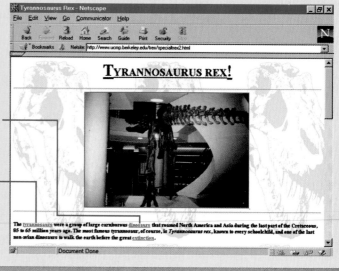

What makes a website special?

A website can combine text, pictures, sound and even video, all connected by links for easy navigation through its pages. Here's a tour around a typical website to show the depth of information available.

Home page ▶

Every website has a home page, rather like the contents page of a magazine or book, which contains hyperlinks to other pages of information on the site.

The website has its own unique address on the Internet, which will look something like: http://www.travelocity.com. You simply type this address into your Web browser to go to that site. If you see a link on a page, you don't even need to type an address, just click on it.

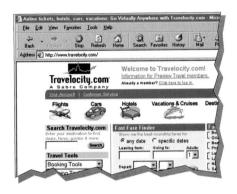

Multimedia ▼

Websites need not look like static magazine pages – many sites have video and sound clips. This travel site even has short videos of many of the most popular tourist destinations from around the world. You select the destination and the video clip is shown as part of the next Web page.

Text ▼

A good website is more than just lots of pictures and hyperlinks. It can be jam-packed with in-depth articles and features – there are no paper costs to worry about, after all. The Travelocity site has lots of travelogs and tourist information.

Downloads ▶

In addition to the Web pages you browse through, many sites have goodies for you to copy from the site to your PC, a process known as downloading. This is a popular way of getting new software for your PC.

Forms ▶

Some Web pages are designed as simple forms. Here you can type in the place you're interested in, click the Map It! button and the website will draw a map and send it to you as the next Web page. You can then save it.

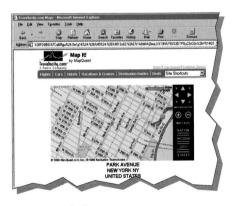

Interactivity ▲

Some websites hardly look like their paper-based equivalents. This map site works just as if it were a computer program running on your PC. You can zoom in and out, go north, east, west and south. All this is chieved using the powerful computer you are accessing.

Advertising banner ▶

Many websites carry advertising. If you want to go to the advertiser's site, just click on the banner.

Email ▶

Some links on a Web page are for sending email. An email address looks something like: name@place.com (the @ symbol stands for 'at').

Click on an email address and your Internet email program will start, ready for you to type your message.

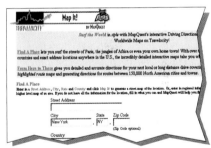

WHAT IT MEANS

HYPERLINKS

Hyperlinks, or links, are the most important part of the World Wide Web. These are items you can click on to move to another page. The website designer can make a site as interactive as necessary using hyperlinks.

Some hyperlinks look like underlined text of a different color, often blue. Links can also be part of, or all of, a picture, or small buttons like the icons in Windows. You can tell which parts of the page are links because the normal mouse pointer changes to a pointing hand when it passes over them.

What you need to get on the Internet

You want to get on the information superhighway, but you're not sure where to begin and you're afraid of the cost. Here's our easy guide to what you need to get connected and how to understand Internet expenses.

D on't worry if it seems like the rest of the world is on the Internet and you've been left behind. Internet users are only a small, but rapidly growing, group of people. Over the next few pages, we're going to tackle the two major obstacles that stop people from becoming part of the Internet community: the jargon, and the question that initially puts a lot of people off, how much the whole operation will cost.

On pages 136–137, we'll look at how easy it is to get online and how much it costs to stay connected. First, though, let's tackle the question of

WHAT IT MEANS

BIT

Short for binary digit, the bit is the smallest unit of information on your PC. Every piece of information computers use and store is converted into a sequence of bits. For example, there are 8 bits in a byte and a CD-ROM contains over 650 million bytes, or more than 5,200,000,000 bits.

A modem and Internet connection will open interesting doors all around the world for you and your family, including news, games, sports and email. Every day Internet access is becoming easier and less expensive.

what type of equipment you'll need to get started.

● Essential equipment

The essentials are a computer and a telephone line – you probably already have these – and a modem. A modem is a device that can send and receive computer data through the telephone line. If you bought your PC recently, you might already have a built-in modem – check the documents that came with your PC.

If you don't have a modem, you can add one to your PC very easily. The most important consideration when choosing a modem is the speed at which it can send and receive data.

This is usually measured in bits per second (bps). The higher the value, the faster the modem, and the faster it operates, the shorter the time you need to spend online.

Most of today's modems operate at 56,000bps, with older ones operating at 33,600bps or even 28,800bps. Modems are relatively cheap, so it is practical to get the fastest available.

If you've got a telephone, you've got a route to the Internet. With a special device, called a modem, your computer connects right to a normal telephone jack.

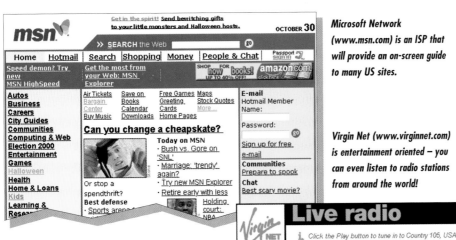

Microsoft Network (www.msn.com) is an ISP that will provide an on-screen guide to many US sites.

Virgin Net (www.virginnet.com) is entertainment oriented – you can even listen to radio stations from around the world!

● At your service

To connect to the Internet you will need to join an Internet service provider (ISP). This is an organization that has computers permanently attached to the Internet, so that when you want to go online, your PC uses your modem to contact their computers. Once connected, your PC becomes part of the Internet.

Traditionally, ISPs all used to be specialized companies charging you a monthly fee (typically about $20) to use their service. Some simply provided software, a connection to the Internet and an email service. But others – notably CompuServe and AOL – also supplied organized content and services, at a slightly higher price. It was up to you whether you simply wanted a means of diving into the Internet or whether you preferred the more structured experience offered by these online services.

But as both the PC and the Internet have become much more of a

mass-market phenomenon, some ISPs have sprung up offering completely free service or now more often a limited number of free hours per month. Others offer a free trial period. But it will be up to you to watch for the expiration date if you decide to cancel the arrangement. Otherwise, payment may automatically be charged to your credit-card account if you provided details when first signing up. The distinction between an ISP pure and simple and an online service has broadly been eroded; nowadays, most

ISPs themselves provide some sort of news, entertainment and shopping service at their own website. On pages 136–137 we'll take a look at some of the different ISPs, and the pros and cons of a free service versus a subscription.

● Name and number

You sign up for a service either by using your PC and modem to dial the ISP's number and following the instructions on screen, or by installing the necessary software from a CD which you can buy in a store or have sent to you. When connecting to some ISPs you might have to enter credit-card details for billing.

The most important aspects to consider when you sign up are your user name and your password. Your user name is the name you will have on the Internet and which people use to send you email. Choose a name carefully (beware of joke names you might regret later) and have some alternatives ready in case your preferred name is already taken.

You will need to remember your user name and password every time you go online. Keep your password secret – anyone who knows it could use your account and peek at your private email. Your ISP will also provide you with Internet software, including an email program and a World Wide Web browser.

Home (www.home.com) has points of presence in the USA and Canada, and combines the depth of search engine Excite with full-motion video and audio.

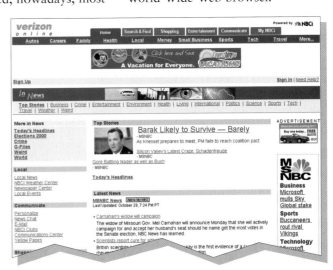

Verizon Online (www.gte.net) is one of the many ISPs that provide an excellent, regularly updated news service.

Which ISP?

Here we take a look at some of the different types of Internet service providers that are available – and the real costs involved.

THE MAJOR decision in choosing an ISP these days is whether to go for a free or a subscription service. That makes your choice sound easy, but things aren't quite as simple as that, for there are several other factors that you should bear in mind in addition to cost.

Both free and subscription ISPs work in pretty much the same way, typically giving you all the necessary software to access the Internet and email services, a number of email addresses (usually five or six of them), and space on their computers for your own website. You may wonder how the free ISPs make a profit, but of course they receive considerable revenue from advertising on their site.

If you do opt for a free ISP, you should remember to keep the account active. This is because most free services reserve the right to terminate your account if you do not use the service for an extended period.

There are usually two billing methods used for ISPs that charge – flat rates and metered rates. Flat rate accounts charge a set amount for unlimited monthly access to the

provider's services. This monthly rate is generally in the region of $20. Metered rate accounts charge a smaller monthly fee for a set number of hours of Internet usage, and a per hour rate after that.

If you're planning to connect to the Web, don't settle for less than a 56K modem. They can be bought for less than $100 and will save you a lot of time in the long run when compared with slower models.

Home users tend to subscribe to a dial-up service from the ISP they select. This means that they call up the ISP's system each time they require connection to the Internet.

Some heavy users, however, prefer to choose a dedicated line service, but this is more expensive.

The following are questions suggested by the Better Business Bureau that you may want to ask an ISP before making your decision.
• If it is likely that you will need access when traveling, find out whether an ISP has local access numbers in other locations.
• Are free trial periods available?
• Has the ISP any software to provide secure shopping and credit-card transactions over the Internet?
• Does the ISP offer technical support at all times?

Whichever ISP you choose, remember that you can always change it if you find the service unsatisfactory. You just download and install new software – but you will have to change your email address.

You can reach the Better Business Bureau on www.newyork.bbb.org for an interesting survey of 30 ISPs and a comparison of their services. Their conclusion is that shopping around will get you the best value for your money. If you ever have need to file a complaint, they suggest you contact the Better Business Bureau in the area where the ISP is located.

AOL AND COMPUSERVE

America Online (AOL) and CompuServe are two of the biggest ISPs in the world. AOL, for example, has around 23 million users worldwide. It provides a different approach from many ISPs. Its service gives you a structured approach to the Internet, providing 'channels' with content related to particular subject areas. It is also strong on forums, where users can exchange ideas and advice. AOL's computer forum, for instance, allows you to discuss topics ranging from 3D graphics cards to virus protection. A lot of the content is unavailable elsewhere, which explains why it is a subscription service. See page 137 for more information about AOL.

Until recently, AOL and CompuServe were competitors among ISPs. (Remember that there are hundreds of ISPs, all of them competing for your business, which is why it is advisable to choose care-fully for the best deal. You may even choose to have two ISPs, one free and one that charges.) But AOL now owns CompuServe. As a result, the two services tend to be differentiated, with AOL targeted principally at the home user and CompuServe aimed more at the business community.

Two of the biggest Internet service providers decided to stop competing with each other and amalgamate and differentiate. AOL now provides services aimed at the home and individual user, while CompuServe targets the business community.

America OnLine

www.aol.com

At the time of going to press, AOL, one of the largest ISPs, is offering 1,000 hours free in your first month after signing on, and the facility to cancel before this period expires. Seven email addresses are offered. There is an unlimited access charge of $23.90 per month. Applicants must be 18 or older, and a major credit card or checking account is required.

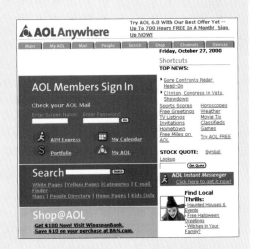

AT&T WorldNet

www.att.net

This Internet service provider has access coverage for over 80 percent of the USA. The monthly charge is $16.95 for 150 hours; $21.95 for unlimited use. It also offers a free one-year subscription to child safety software for safe surfing.

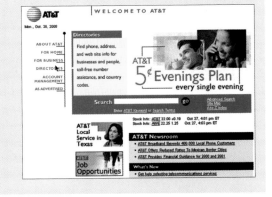

Earthlink

www.earthlink.net

This company provides dial-up access from over 1,300 locations nationwide and claims to be the second largest ISP in the US, having merged with Mindspring in February 2000. There is a setup fee of $25 and a monthly charge of $19.95, but special offers are sometimes available for the first six months.

Inter.net

www.inter.net

One of the largest ISPs, Inter.net provides continual toll-free technical support. The setup fee is $20 (waived if you sign up online), and there is a $19.95 monthly charge for an individual, with special rates for a family.

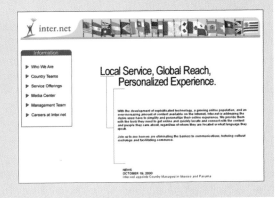

Net Zero

www.netzero.net

This is an example of a completely free ISP, as long as your usage is below 10 hours a month. After installing the program, you will be able to access the Internet from most cities in the USA or Canada. You will find when using the service that an advertising banner regularly appears but it can be moved very easily to make it as unobtrusive as possible.

PC TIPS

Netiquette

There is a code of conduct for correct use of the Internet that is now called *netiquette*. As you might guess, it is derived from the word *etiquette*. This is generally an unwritten code, but some ISPs will suggest in their terms and conditions that you follow certain specific guidelines, such as the following, to make sure that no embarrassing situations or other types of problems arise.

• Don't send any messages, data, images, or programs that could be libelous, defamatory, obscene, threatening, abusive, rude, or hateful.

• Don't send viruses or any other destructive elements.

• Take care not to infringe any copyrights or trademarks.

The above are not only abuses of *netiquette*, but can be criminal offenses.

Setting up a modem

To get onto the Internet, you must first add a modem to your PC. These devices come in many shapes and sizes, but they all do the same job – sending computer signals down the telephone line.

A modem is a device that connects your PC to the telephone network, and, therefore, potentially to any other computer that is also connected to the telephone network, anywhere in the world.

Adding a modem (assuming that your PC doesn't already have one built in) allows you to access the Internet, send and receive email and faxes and link with other PCs to transfer information or play games. Some modern modems can even act as telephone answering machines.

● **Buying decisions**

If you want to use your modem to connect to the Internet, you will have to open an account with an Internet service provider (see ISP, pages 136–137). For hardware, you need only the modem itself, although you do need to connect it to your telephone line.

It is easy to plug your modem into your existing phone line using a 'splitter' plug, which works much like the adaptor you use to plug more than two appliances into an electrical outlet. Modems come with quite long cords, and this might result in long cables trailing from the nearest phone jack to your computer desk.

If this is the case, you might need to think about installing an extra telephone jack – either by using a kit or getting your telephone company to put one in. Remember, if you only have one telephone line,

Modems such as the Hayes Accura (shown right) can distinguish between faxes and voice calls automatically.

Modems can be external to the PC or fitted inside the casing. Internal types need far less cabling.

you can't make telephone calls while you are using the Internet, so it could be worth thinking about getting an extra phone line.

● **Choosing a modem**

An extra line also means you can let the modem answer incoming calls automatically. This is very convenient, but on a shared line it means that anyone calling you from a normal telephone will be answered by a beeping modem (note: some modems can distinguish between different kinds of transmission, see opposite).

As with any piece of hardware, there are several choices to be made when buying a modem.

HOW YOUR MODEM WORKS

A modem works by converting the digital information that a computer deals with into an analog signal that can be sent down the phone line. It 'modulates' data going into the phone network so it becomes a series of whistles and bleeps, and 'demodulates' the signal coming out back into digital bits – hence the name 'modem', which is short for MOdulate/ DEModulate. If you find these concepts a bit confusing, don't worry; you're not alone, and your modem will work just fine anyway!

The specifications vary as much as for any hardware and will affect the price. The most important factor is speed, and most modems sold today are fast 56,600bps models. A modem of this speed, from a well-known manufacturer, such as US Robotics or Motorola, will typically cost less than $100.

There are several key aspects to consider when choosing a modem for use at home. Let's go through them one by one.

● Modem speed

The faster your modem can go, the less time it takes to transmit data, saving you time and frustration. After a while, these savings often cover the high initial purchase cost. Modem speed is measured in bits per second (bps) or sometimes kilobits per second (kbps). Currently, the fastest modems for PCs work at 56,600bps (or 56.6kbps). However, you should be aware that this figure is slightly misleading. The highest speeds can be reached only with one-way traffic – either sending or receiving data – and this doesn't happen all the time. Also, your modem can transmit and receive only

at the same speed of the modem at the other end of the telephone line. At the moment, 56,600bps modems are the fastest modems you can buy, and it's unlikely that faster modems will come along (for an alternative, see Going Digital, below).

However, you might come across other modems in the bargain bin at your local computer shop. These may run at 33,600bps or even 28,800bps. No matter how cheap these modems seem, they are a false economy: because of the extra time you spend online, you end up paying more in time lost than you save in the initial purchase.

● External and internal

There are two main types of modem: internal and external. An external modem is usually about the size of a VHS videocassette and sits on your desk. It has two connectors: one for the cable to the PC's 'COM' (short for communications) port and one for the cable to the phone jack. There will also be a power-supply socket. The newer PCs also have a USB (Universal Serial Bus) socket to which USB modems can link. An internal modem fits inside your PC. The advantage of internal modems is that they don't take up desk space, and they can be cheaper than external models. However, they are much trickier to install: you have to open up your computer and plug the modem into the right slot, which can be a daunting prospect. On balance, the external modem is the best bet for most people.

This Pace V90 modem connects to the latest USB socket.

● Fax/modems

The ability to send and receive faxes is a standard feature on most modern modems, but it's wise to check just in case. Modems that can handle faxes are called fax/modems.

Bear in mind that, unlike a fax machine, modems deal with computer

Add a fax/modem to your PC and anyone anywhere in the world can send a fax straight to you. Better still, you can send faxes directly from your PC.

documents. So it's easy to send a letter you have created on your PC – you can fax it in much the same way as you would send it to the printer. But to send a paper document (perhaps a form you have filled in by hand), you must get it onto your PC to fax it, and that requires another device – a scanner (we'll cover these later in the course). When you receive a fax, you can view it on screen, but to see it on paper you will have to print it out.

● Extra phone features

Some modems can also handle voice messages, rather like an answering machine. Others have sophisticated voice-mail features, so each member of the family can have a personal message mailbox, with messages stored on the PC's hard disk.

These capabilities are handy if you have only one telephone line: the modem can tell the difference between an incoming fax or voice call, and receive and record each one accordingly. To fully exploit the fax and phone facilities of most modems, you need to leave the PC and modem switched on all the time.

Many modems come as part of a package, with free fax software, games and special offers for Internet connection. Shop around.

GOING DIGITAL

For faster speeds, you could get an ADSL (Asymmetrical Digital Subscriber Link) – commonly known as DSL, an all-digital line giving you a permanent connection to the Internet. Speeds vary depending on which RBOC (Regional Bell Operating Company) services your area, and not all areas have access. But at a typical 512,000bps for downloads and 256,000 for uploads (publishing pages on the Internet) it's much faster than a modem.

There are other benefits too. As long as the computer and DSL device are turned on, DSL connections are constant. You pay only a fixed monthly fee. Contact your local telephone provider and ask for details on ADSL.

Connecting your modem

Connecting your computer to the outside world seems a daunting prospect, but there are only four connections to make, and by following these simple steps you will be ready to get online in minutes.

ALL PCs have a bank of sockets (or ports) on their reverse, so you'll have to clear enough space to get access to the rear of your PC.

After switching the PC off, put all of the items – modem, modem cable, phone wire and power supply – in rough positions between your PC and the electrical outlet and phone jack. If the cables are not long enough, you'll need an extension for the phone or power cord.

● **Cables and connectors**

There's a chance that your modem cable has the wrong-size plug – for example, a smaller 9-pin plug where your PC's COM port has 25 pins. You can either buy a new cable or a small 9–25-pin adaptor. If you don't already have a spare telephone jack, you can buy a splitter from a home store.

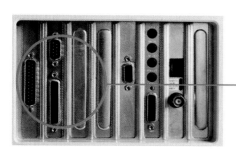

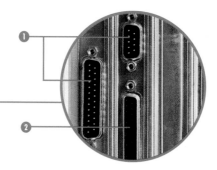

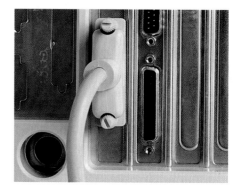

1 First locate the COM (communications) ports: look at the back of your PC and find the sockets circled above. In our illustration, the COM ports are labeled ❶. The other port ❷ is the parallel port, usually used for connecting to a printer. You might find that one of your COM ports is already being used, perhaps for your mouse, but that's no problem: you can use either for a modem.

2 Plug one end of the modem cable into the 25-pin COM connector on the back of the computer and tighten the two securing screws at each side.

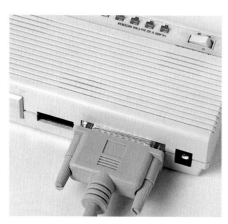

3 Plug the other end of the modem cable into the 25-pin COM port on the back of the modem. To guarantee a good connection, gently tighten the two securing screws.

4 Modems normally have a separate external power adaptor. Plug this into an electrical outlet and plug the cable into the back of the modem itself, but do not turn the modem on for the moment.

5 Take the phone line from the modem and plug it into the phone jack. Switch on the modem and the PC. Now you're ready to install the modem software. This is covered step by step on the opposite page.

Modem software setup

Once connected, a simple installation gets your PC and modem working.

WHEN YOU restart your PC you might find that Windows recognizes that a new device has been added. It will find it and then prompt you with simple on-screen instructions. Don't worry if Windows doesn't spot your modem immediately; there are new products coming onto the market all the time and Windows can't have up-to-date information about every single new modem. If this is the case, you can install the modem yourself.

Windows will help with its Install New Modem wizard, which makes the installation an almost automatic procedure. But keep your modem manual handy along with any disks that were supplied.

1 Double-click on the Control Panel icon and a window like the one below will pop up. (Note: depending on the software installed on your PC, you might have some extra icons and/or slightly different icons for a few of the programs.) Find the Modems icon, which looks like a telephone on top of a gray box. Double-click this icon with the left mouse button.

2 The Modems Properties box now appears. No modem is currently set up, so click with the left mouse button on the Add button to start the installation procedure.

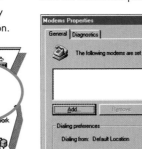

3 Now the Install New Modem wizard appears to guide you through the process. Make sure the modem is turned on and then click on the Next button.

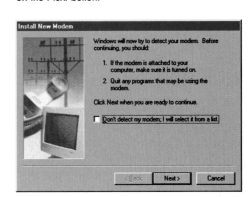

4 Windows will take a few moments to search for the modem before actually detecting it. If Windows has correctly identified the modem, just click Next.

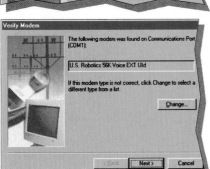

5 Windows tells you the modem is now installed, and all you have to do is click Finish to end the process.

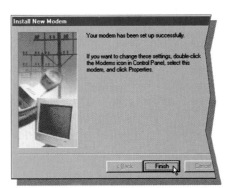

6 If Windows has incorrectly identified your modem, click the Change button to select a different model. A list of manufacturers and models is supplied. Use the scroll bar to the right of the list of manufacturers to select a modem maker. When you find the maker of your modem, click on it and then use the list on the right to select the particular model. If your modem is on the list, then just click on it and end the process as in step 5.

7 If your modem came with a CD-ROM, it might contain useful communications software. To install such software, insert the CD into your PC's CD-ROM drive and follow the on-screen instructions. You might get answering machine software and extra fax features.

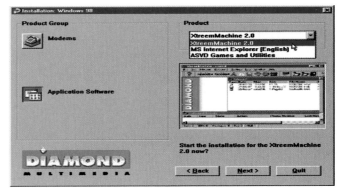

The X Files and the Unexplained

From the bizarre to the disturbing, paranormal phenomena are always hard to pin down. But thanks to the global access offered by the Internet, the answers are out there – somewhere.

A television program can't be doing too badly in the popularity stakes when it manages to outdo the turn of the millennium in terms of its influence on the public worldwide. For although the arrival of the year 2000 was undoubtedly behind the surge of interest in the paranormal and the spiritual, it is *The X Files* that focused this fascination and made it fashionable in the buildup and after.

For those few who have managed to avoid the show's charms, its premise is quite simple. Hotshot FBI agent Fox Mulder is in charge of the 'X Files' – a series of unsolved cases which appear to have no logical solution, but in some way involve paranormal phenomena.

Although the FBI tolerates Mulder's passion – which is fueled by his sister's apparent abduction by aliens when he was young – unidentified factions within the government (and beyond) are less happy. In order to debunk Mulder's findings, agent Dana Scully, who has a scientific background, is assigned as his partner so that she can report on the validity of his work. The pair then proceed to combat (with varying degrees of

success) government conspiracies, UFOs, aliens, ghosts, demons, serial killers and everything in between.

This might not immediately sound like a ticket to mass-market appeal, but a combination of excellent acting, writing, direction and deadpan black humor – plus a couple of attractive stars – has resulted not only in impressive viewing figures and a generation of X Philes, but also a fistful of awards.

● Made for the Net
Of course, the combination of TV brand loyalty, bizarre subject matter and good-looking actors is perfect for the wacky world of the Internet. This has led to a veritable invasion of *X Files* websites, which only adds to an enormous number of 'ordinary' sites dealing with the unexplained.

Some of the latter have obviously been around longer and might cover an almost infinite range of subjects. However, they usually fall into one of three broad groups: the reasonably scientific and organized; the amateurish and illogical – but undoubtedly enthusiastic; and the downright bizarre.

Each category is entertaining in its own way, but you should be careful of the particularly odd sites, as these can be

strange to the point of unpleasantness or even illegality.

For that reason, it is always best to keep an eye on children when they look at such sites, and to restrict browsing to some of the more responsible sites.

Fox Mulder (far right) investigates the weird and wonderful reports involving anything paranormal, while Dana Scully (near right) applies a more scientific approach, reporting to her bosses on the facts as she sees them.

WHAT IT MEANS

X PHILES

Really obsessive TV and movie fans love to give themselves a name that describes their allegiance, the infamous Trekkies and Whovians being perhaps the most familiar.

Continuing this trend, many pun-loving X Files *fans like to refer to themselves as* X Philes. *So don't be alarmed if you see this term used on any of these websites…it's not a spelling error.*

Exploring the Unexplained on the Internet

**The truth is out there – and also the not-so-true.
Visit these sites to make up your own mind.**

The Official X Files Website
www.fox.com/thexfiles

Supported by the makers of the TV series, the biggest and most impressive section of this site is the guide to each series of the show, split up into all its episodes. Each episode is described in some detail and has an accompanying photo, video clip, audio file and credits list. Other sections of the site give biographies of the actors, information on the making of the show and a forum for fans to exchange views.

Circlemakers
www.circlemakers.org

This is a curious, not to say weird, site for a variety of different reasons. First of all, it's about the crop circle phenomenon – a relatively new area of weirdness that took off in the last two decades of the 20th century. Second, it appears to be put together by a bunch of people whose aim seems to be to debunk the whole thing – which they do by going around and creating their very own elaborate crop circles. On this extremely stylish and witty site, you can see their and others' handiwork, and, as they put it, 'gain some insight into why this tight band of individuals spend their summers out in the fields of England flattening cereal crops in various intricate patterns'. There's plenty of 'evidence' in the form of photos and real audio files. It's a very odd site, but well worth a look.

The GATB
www.gatb.org

Few X Philes (see opposite page) can claim that their enthusiasm for the show is restricted to an academic interest in the subject matter, or an admiration of the cinematography. For although not everyone will agree as to whether the two main actors rate as classical beauties, they have both managed to become international sex symbols. There are many sites dedicated to David Duchovny and Gillian Anderson, although not usually to both of them at the same time. The GATB stands for Gillian Anderson Testosterone Brigade, and is one of the main ports of call for the Scully-obsessed.

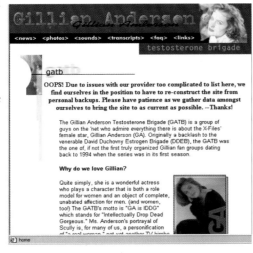

Fortean Times
www.forteantimes.com

Charles Fort was an intellectual who wrote books about science and the unexplained during the 1930s. Fort observed that much research was anything but scientific, noting that inconvenient data was often suppressed or avoided. He thus became convinced that there was much in the world that could not be explained by traditional science, and he sought to document it in a magazine called *Fortean Times*. This has become widely read and the related website features some of its stories and pictures. The site has a good links page and an online form for reporting weird sightings and stories.

Anomalist
www.anomalist.com

The Anomalist is another Web-based version of a printed magazine, which is not dissimilar to *Fortean Times*. The publication certainly shares the same admiration for Charles Fort and his musings, but the Anomalist website distinguishes itself from that of Fortean Times by having a smaller number of longer articles. These cover topics from UFO sightings to Bigfoots. Every story is taken seriously, even though it might be related with a large degree of knowing humor. For the Anomalist site, the truth behind a hoaxed paranormal event is just as interesting as vague facts about a 'real' sighting, since both kinds reveal more about human nature than they ever do about how many humps the Loch Ness monster really has.

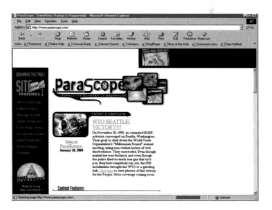

The Parascope
www.parascope.com

This site is, in many ways, the American equivalent to something like the British Fortean Times or Anomalist websites. However, it's a little less 'serious' and, at the same time, all too eager to believe the most ludicrous of paranormal theories. In truth, there is little actual attempt to explain or theorize on any of the stories reported, but it's quite clear that the writers tend more toward the conspiratorial view of things than accepting the innocent explanation. But this hardly seems to matter as the site doesn't really expect anyone to come here looking for rigorous scientific debate, but rather for an amusing or spooky story.

CSETI
www.cseti.com

CSETI is short for the Center for the Study of Extraterrestrial Intelligence, which all sounds terribly official and governmental, but it's not. It's an organization founded and run by a medical doctor, Steven Greer, who says CSETI is 'the only worldwide organization dedicated to establishing peaceful and sustainable relations with extraterrestrial lifeforms'. There's material on Greer himself ('widely regarded as the world's leading authority on the subject of extraterrestrial intelligence'), field reports of 'sightings', information on where to spot satellites and details of the RMIT – the Rapid Mobilization Investigative Team.

BUFORA Online
www.bufora.org.uk

There are UFO investigation groups all over the world and many have websites. The British Unidentified Flying Object Research Association (BUFORA), for example, is the UK's biggest such organization and is closely affiliated with similar groups around the world. Its website is large and well worth a visit. It is split into several main areas: a News section, featuring UFO case studies, opinions and breaking news; a Research section, where sightings are reported and similar observations can be studied; an Investigations section, where current UFO-seeking is documented; and a Members Only section.

SITES TO @ VISIT

There is certainly no shortage of unexplained sites on the Web, so here's a selection from the best of the rest:

News of the Weird
www.newsoftheweird.com

Chuck Shepard's News of the Weird is a collection of strange news clippings from around the world. There's no attempt at verification or explanation; you're meant to read and be amused by the things culled from the small print of every paper under the sun.

Weird Science
www.eskimo.com/~billb/weird.html

Not so much a site in itself as an extensive collection of articles and links to other sites, all of which attempt to put some wonder back into science. There's stuff on 'scientists' transcended experiences' and well-known but little understood phenomena, such as Tesla coils and ball lightning. Following just a few of the links in the site's long list could shake the convictions of even the most hardened of skeptics.

Weird History 101
www.thegrid.net/fern.canyon/weird/history.htm

This amusing little site is really a teaser to get you to buy the book of the same name. You get lots of snippets of wild and wacky facts of history, and a sample from the book recounting some of the more bizarre acts, habits and sayings of presidents, one of whom – perhaps talking of the paranormal – apparently said, 'I have opinions of my own – strong opinions – but I don't always agree with them.'

The Science Behind the _X Files_ HYPERLINK
huah.net/scixf

This is a fascinating site, the author of which has a scientific background. It attempts to cover each episode of the TV program, commenting on all the scientific and paranormal events featured, complete with possible solutions. What makes this process interesting is that each comment is backed up with a hyperlink to a relevant website, allowing you to research for yourself.

Conspire.com
www.conspire.com

On the surface, it doesn't really seem that conspiracies – whether committed by big business or the government – have much to do with the world of the unexplained or paranormal. But _The X Files_ forged a link, so the paranoid world of conspiracies has become synonymous with that of ghosts, ghouls and aliens.

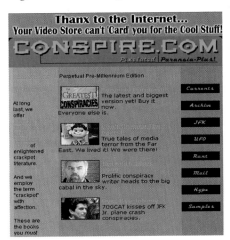

Conspiracy theories can often be depressing and disagreeable, so it's refreshing to come across this site, which takes the whole thing with a pinch of salt. Conspire.com comprises separate sections labeled UFOlogy, JFKology and Rant, which, as well as being informative, together manage to put the fun back into apocalyptic global conspiracies.

Cryptozoology!
www.ncf.carleton.ca/~bz050/HomePage.cryptoz.html

The term 'cryptozoology' was coined in 1959 to describe the search for (and research into) previously unknown animals. To many this might just imply treks in search of the Yeti or Loch Ness Monster, but, in fact, it has a much more mainstream application in identifying new species of insects, birds and mammals.

Of course, many people involved in this sort of research still dream of dissecting Nessie or caging Bigfoot, but no doubt prefer to keep this side of things quiet when talking to more conventional scientists.

This site is therefore a mixture of descriptions and pictures of everything

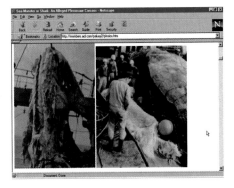

from a new kind of beetle with strange joints in its legs, to an amazing picture of what might or might not turn out to be the Abominable Snowman.

Recent sightings of 'large black cats' in remote parts of Britain have excited cryptozoologists, and the site has an extensive section on these.

Obiwan's UFO-free Paranormal Page
www.ghosts.org

This site concerns what used to be the major focus of paranormal research: ghosts and the supernatural. The graphics aren't as good as some websites, but there is an impressive range of content. Most amusing is the list of haunted hotels, complete with booking rates and tourist information.

There's also a large database of supposedly true ghost stories, sent in by visitors to the site. To top things off there's a huge page with links to ghost investigators, case studies and just about anything else that goes bump in the night.

Connecting to AOL

AOL is one of the world's largest suppliers of online services. We show you what you can expect to find if you join, how easy it is to connect for the first time and where you can get the AOL software.

The initials AOL stand for America Online. Despite the name, it's a global Internet service provider with around 23 million members that supplies a lot of exclusive online services for its subscribers.

This members-only service also provides Internet email – so you can keep in touch with other Internet users. To connect to the Internet and World Wide Web, you use the customized Web browser which is included in the AOL package.

● One-button browsing

AOL aims to make it simple for non-expert users to get on the Internet. To access the Internet via AOL, all you do is click on the Internet button and then choose the option you want from the next screen. You can browse the Web, download files, access news groups and more besides. There's even space for you to build your own Web pages.

AOL's member services are split into a number of different subject areas (or channels); these include Business and Careers, Travel, Computing, Personal Finance, Health, Entertainment, News, Sports, Games, Local City Guides and Women. There's also a Chat area where you can have live online conversations with other AOL

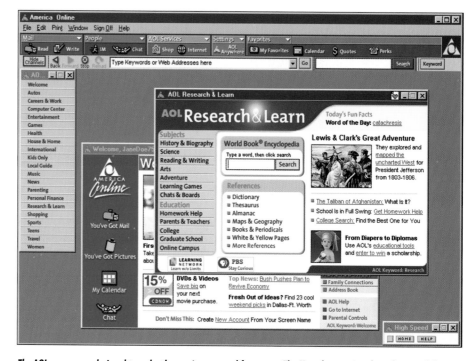

The AOL screens are designed to make the service easy and fun to use. The Menu bar running along the top of the screen travels with you from area to area, so you quickly get the hang of navigating your way around.

users. On pages 148–149, we take a look at some of these areas in more detail and give examples of what AOL has to offer.

● Try before you buy

Internet service providers compete very fiercely; the good news is that you can try AOL's services before committing yourself. You'll need to get a copy of the AOL program, but AOL will send you a free CD-ROM (see Try an AOL free trial, right). Of course, you'll need a modem so that you can connect to AOL.

You then need to work through the setup program. Opposite, we show you how to get connected for the first time. The process is the same whether you download the software or get it on disk. Once you're signed up, you'll have full access to AOL's complete range of services.

The AOL Internet access screen takes the mystery and uncertainty out of Web browsing. There is online help and easy access to a wealth of features.

PC TIPS

Try an AOL free trial

If you'd like to try out AOL's online services to see if they suit you, you can take advantage of its free 30-day trial. AOL discs are widely available at electronic stores. Or you can telephone AOL at 800-827-6364 and request a free copy of the software.

If you already have a connection to the Internet, you can also visit AOL's Web site at www.aol.com where you can download the installation software for free and find out how to use it. However, be warned: the installation software is over 10 MB and it will take a long time to download to your computer. You might find it easier to order the CD-ROM by telephone. If you don't wish to continue using AOL after the trial period, simply telephone the company and cancel your account.

Connecting to AOL for the first time

There are many different types of Internet service provider and connecting to any requires a modem and access to a phone line. Here, we show you how to join AOL using one of its connection CD-ROMs.

1 First, place the AOL CD-ROM in your CD-ROM drive. The program will start automatically. The first screen you see asks whether you are joining as a new member or are just upgrading. Select the New Member option and then click Next.

2 You will have to wait for a few minutes while the software checks to see if any previous versions are installed on your hard disk. Then you are asked which directory you want to install the software in; it's best to accept the suggested default and click on Next. The necessary files are now copied from the CD-ROM to your computer's hard disk.

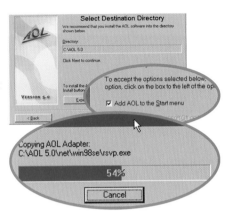

3 Once the file copying process is complete, the AOL installation software needs to restart Windows for the changes to take effect. Click the Restart Now button.

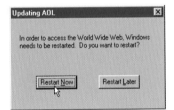

4 You are offered two installation options; click the option for Begin automatic setup and then the Next icon to continue. At this stage make sure your modem is switched on and connected, and also that Windows knows the modem is there (see pages 140–141). The AOL software searches for the modem and identifies it. If your model of modem is not highlighted, select the Change Modem icon to look for it.

5 Once the software has correctly identified your modem, click Next. Choose the phone numbers for connecting to AOL. Make sure United States is selected. Let the AOL software go online and pick up the list of access numbers. Choose two numbers by checking their boxes then click Next. AOL shows you the phone numbers and confirms dialing instructions. Click the Next button to connect to AOL.

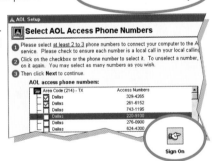

6 The software now dials the selected number to connect you to AOL. Select the top option and fill in the registration number and password printed on the CD packaging. Then fill in the personal details on the next screen, and on the one after choose your credit/debit card payment method and fill in the details.

7 You now need to choose a screen name – the name you will use for email and by which you will be known online. Once you've done this, you also need to choose a password, which you confirm by typing it in twice. Then click Continue.

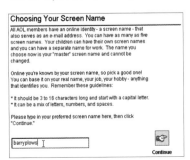

8 You're now a member, as you'll see from the AOL Welcome screen that appears, and the fact that email is awaiting your attention.

What you will find on AOL

You can start browsing around AOL's sites and services right away. Here we take a look at some of the most popular ones.

AOL HAS ITS own organized areas that are out of bounds for other Internet users. For new users, these areas are ideal, as they are navigated by point and click operations, which are familiar to Windows users. You don't need to know any Web addresses or anything about search engines when you start; you can learn about these things at your own pace when you feel comfortable in the AOL areas. We've taken a look at seven of the most popular areas (or channels) on this page and the next.

DIGITAL CITY

Through AOL, you can get the lowdown on what's happening not only in your own locality and across the United States, but also worldwide. Say, for example, you are planning a tour of the UK. Just click on the relevant area of the map and you'll get listings ranging from an Insider's Guide to Wales to a webcam bringing coverage of tourist attractions and unusual places of interest in London.

A number of major cities, such as Dallas-Fort Worth, get their own sub-channels with links to activities and restaurant listings, for example, within their respective regional sections.

NEWS

This is the place to find the latest news stories. There are links to the day's headline reports and connections to news information from respected sources, such as the Associated Press and CNN. You can check out specialist sections for sports and financial news, or focus on home news or international reports. The News on the Web section gives you links to the thousands of news websites all around the world, including locations as diverse as Australia, Hong Kong, Sweden, Brazil and Zambia.

SPORTS

The Sports channel supplies comprehensive coverage of just about every major sporting activity in separate subchannels. You'll find features, results, match reports and more. There's also, of course, top-level latest news of the whole sporting world. There's plenty of interactive fun offered as well. You can try out the baseball management simulation, enter the sports caption contest, take part in the lively forums and discussions, and enter competitions to win tickets to top events. In fact, there's something for everyone.

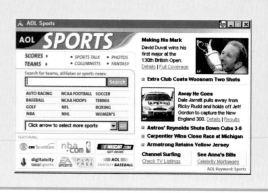

ENTERTAINMENT

You can find a vast amount of show-business news and gossip on the channel devoted to the world of entertainment. There are sections covering film, television, music, the arts and culture. There's also a Cult section where fans of science fiction and fantasy can find out more about their passions and chat with other fans. The Television section recommends essential viewing each day, while the Arts section even has an interactive Book Club. There are opportunities throughout to win competition prizes.

KIDS

The Kids Only channel is always packed with things to do. There's a resource of links to fun sites for youngsters on the Internet and a direct link to the Kids Only online chat area called Chit Chat. You can also find out about games or choose to go to areas devoted to Girls' Stuff or Boys' Stuff. And Kids Box is an area run in conjunction with the children's television company Nickelodeon, which produces many children's small-screen favorites, including Rugrats, who frequently make an appearance here.

COMPUTING

AOL's Computer Center is densely packed with information and practical advice on just about every aspect of the computer world. You can buy and sell, check out software releases, download lots of useful free programs and browse highlights from the computer press. There's plenty of useful advice plus hints and tips for those who consider themselves beginners; if you don't find what you want here, then post a message in one of the many forums and the chances are that someone will come back with the answer you need.

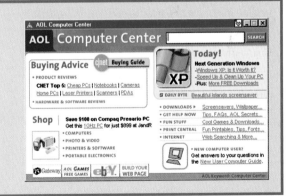

CHAT

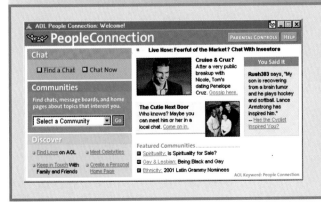

Every one of the AOL channels has a program of hosted live-chat events throughout the week. The subjects covered are extremely varied. For instance, on one evening you could join online discussions about subjects as diverse as baseball, evangelism, foreign languages, your local community and kids' issues. You can view the schedule for the week in advance and if nothing appeals, you can always enter some of the private chat areas, raising any of your favorite topics until you find people who respond to your interests.

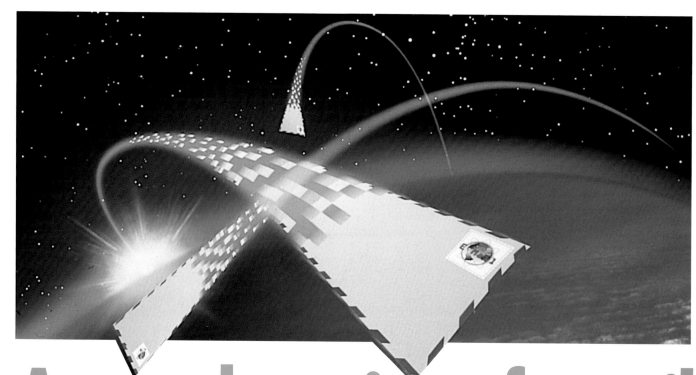

An explanation of email

Wherever you and your PC are, you can send electronic mail, or email, to any other Internet user. You can also send and receive pictures, spreadsheets and other file types – almost instantly.

One of the most exciting aspects of connecting your computer to the Internet is the ability you have to send and receive electronic mail, or 'email'. Everywhere you look you see evidence of how popular email is – alongside telephone numbers and postal addresses for most businesses, there are now also email addresses. Email rivals the World Wide Web as the most popular use of the Internet. At its most basic, email is a fast way to send a written message to someone, but instead of using a pen and paper, typewriter or word processor, you use an email program on your computer to create and send messages.

The main advantages of email are its speed and flexibility: it is possible to send messages from your own PC to anyone in the world who has an email address, and vice versa, in minutes. And it is not only the written word that you can send. You can also dispatch pictures, programs and sound by email. This ability to send data electronically will save you postage or courier costs.

● **The fax of life**
When you send a fax, the recipient's machine could be busy and you will have to tie up your phone line with repeated attempts to get through. In contrast, your email goes instantly via your Internet service provider (ISP) to the ISP of the person you want to contact.

You won't always receive an instant reply, however. Email won't be read until the recipient checks in to download his or her new messages. Therefore, the lightning speed of your email message zooming across the Internet is worthless if the person you are writing to logs on only to check for email once a week! However, most people who use email check for messages regularly and reply quickly.

For families and friends living in different states, email is usually a cheaper and quicker option for sending messages and pictures than the mail.

EMAIL IS CHEAP

The popularity of email is partly due to its speed, but also its cost. Email can be cheap to use, particularly if you regularly keep in contact with far-flung family, friends or business colleagues by telephone. An email is far cheaper than long-distance telephone calls – even when you make the call during the cheap-rate times.

What's in an address?

Email addresses can look confusing at first. Here's a quick guide to the strange world of email addresses and how to read them.

A POSTAL ADDRESS includes a name, street, town, zip code and country. An email address contains different elements to this (see Understanding An Email Address, below). Most have a reference to the person's name, which may be spelled out in full or have an abbreviation of the person's first name or surname.

Next comes the @ symbol, which stands for 'at', followed by the name of the organization 'at' which the person is located.

This organization is usually an Internet service provider (ISP) or a company. It's also known as the domain and is where the recipient of the email has an account. The letters at the end of the domain indicate which type of organization manages the domain and often in which country the domain is based. For example, the letters '.co' shows that the organization is a company, and '.uk' indicates that the organization is based in the United Kingdom.

● **Naming names**
When you decide to connect to the Internet you will have to choose a name to use as part of your email address. It's up to you what you select, but remember that your choice with any given ISP could well be limited by the number of other people who have joined. Every email address with an ISP has to be unique; you don't want email intended for you being sent to another person of the same name!

So, if your name is John Smith it is unlikely that you will be able to have 'johnsmith' as part of your email address. But you can add letters or numbers to make your email name unique. Here we show examples of

One advantage of email is that mailing costs will be eliminated – reduced at most to the cost of a few seconds of a local telephone call.

some of the variations that a person whose name is Mandy Hughes may either expect from, or suggest to, a fictional ISP called 'condor.com.'

**mhughes@condor.com
mandy234@condor.com
mandy.hughes@condor.com
123456.1234@condor.com**

There are a few variations you may come across in email addresses. Instead of '.com', for example, you may see '.org' – this usually stands for a nonprofit organization, such as a charity. Or you may see '.edu', which means 'educational' and refers to an educational institution, such as a university. No matter how a person's email address appears, as long as you enter it correctly into your email program (see next page) the recipient will get your message.

UNDERSTANDING AN EMAIL ADDRESS

1 The name of the person whose email account it is comes first. It may be a full name with the first and second name separated by a period (.), an abbreviation of the first name with the full surname or even a nickname.

2 The @ symbol separates the name of the person from the domain.

3 Next comes the domain name of the organization that stores the email messages for the recipient.

mhughes@condor.com

4 Periods separate the different elements that make up the domain. (There are never any spaces in an email address.)

5 The letters 'com' mean that the organization is a commercial company. (Nonprofit organizations use 'org' and ISPs often use 'net'.)

WHAT IT MEANS

DOMAIN
This is jargon for an Internet site. Often, it's the name of a company, such as microsoft.com. Other times, it's the name of the Internet service provider with which the recipient has an account, such as aol.com.

Sending and receiving email

Your ISP will supply the software you need to send and receive email. Here we look at how to send an email using Microsoft's Outlook Express.

IT'S EASY TO write a short email, click Send and make contact with a friend or relative. Here we show you how to communicate with people using your computer.

Windows 98 includes Internet Explorer, software for browsing the World Wide Web, and Outlook Express, which allows you to send and receive email. We'll use Outlook Express to show you how to send and receive email, but since all email

programs have similar features, you'll be able to apply the steps here to whichever program your ISP supplies, or that you decide to use.

Email software sorts your incoming and outgoing mail, clearly displaying the sender's name and the subject. There are also windows available that display a list of received and sent messages and where you can display and read the contents of your messages.

1 Internet Explorer will have placed a shortcut to Outlook Express on your Desktop. Just double-click on this icon to start the program. You don't actually need to be connected to the Internet while you write your messages.

2 The first time you start Outlook Express you'll receive a message right away from Microsoft, telling you about features of the program. This message appears in the top half of your Inbox screen. To read it, just highlight it with a single click and its contents will appear in the bottom half of the screen. The scroll bar on the right shows there is more to read. Click the scroll buttons to see more, just as you would in a word processor.

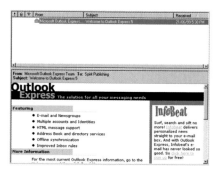

3 To reply to a message, click on the Reply button. This will create a reply window with the address of the person you are replying to already in place. All you have to do is enter the text of the message and click the Send button.

4 To send a new message, click on the New Mail button. Your own email address automatically appears in the From: line. Enter the recipient's address in the To: line and a heading in the Subject: line. Type your message in the main area.

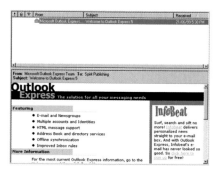

5 You don't want to send the message right now, so select Send Later from the File menu. A window appears telling you that the message will be placed in your Outbox ready to be sent when you choose.

6 When you are online and ready to send all your messages, click on the Send and Receive button. A dialog box will tell you the status of your outgoing and incoming mail. It can be both convenient and efficient to send and receive all your email in one go.

7 You should check at regular intervals to see if you have received any email. Start Outlook Express and click the Send and Receive button. If you have new messages they will appear in your Inbox in the upper half of the screen. Just click on the message and it opens in the bottom half of the screen.

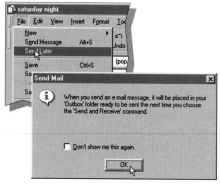

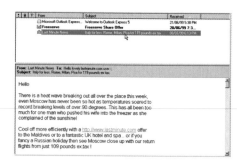

What happens when you send an email

Just as a letter goes from a mailbox to a post office and then on to the delivery address, an email follows an electronic route from your computer to an ISP, where it is 'sorted' and directed to the recipient's computer.

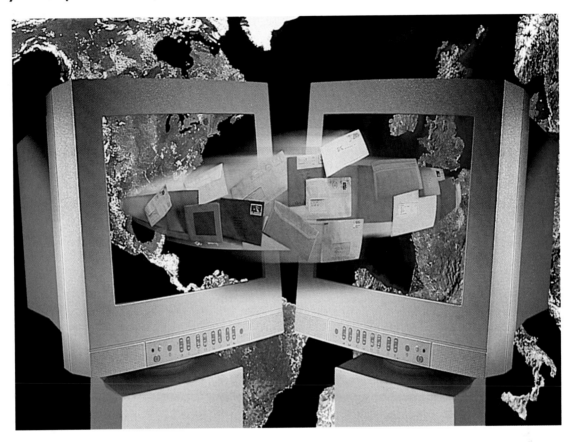

THE FIRST thing that happens to your message when you connect to your ISP to send your email, is that it's converted from the digital data that computers use, to analog waves that telephone lines transmit.

The initial stage of the journey takes the email from your end of the telephone line to the other end. This is the location of your ISP, where there are powerful computers known as mail servers. Rather like a normal post office, this is where the next stage of your email's journey is determined.

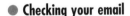
● Checking your email
The ISP's modem and computer converts the analog waves from the telephone line back into digital information and looks at the address you are sending the mail to. It makes sure that the mail was received correctly and then sends the message to the recipient's ISP.

The recipient's ISP receives the mail and places it in a computer mailbox, waiting for the recipient to dial up and collect, as they would with a P.O. Box. When the person you sent the message to dials their ISP, they're automatically notified that email is waiting for them. When they get their mail, their modem receives another analogue signal from the ISP's

Even if your email message is addressed to someone local, the path of the message might involve not only several different computers, but also different countries across the world.

computer. The modem converts this back to digital information and the email message appears – exactly as you sent it – on the screen of the recipient's computer.

EXPRESS YOURSELF WITH EMOTICONS

You might notice that some people include strange groups of characters in their email messages. Look at the messages from the side, and you'll see that they look like little faces. These are called emoticons – short for emotion icons.

Emoticons are used because it's hard to get a tone of voice – happy, sad, angry, etc. – into a text-only email. To help them avoid misunderstandings, particularly when people didn't understand that a

comment was a joke, early computer users devised a shorthand way of being more expressive.

They used normal text characters to create icons. The first was a 'smiley,' created by a colon, a dash and a right parenthesis. Together they look like this :-) which means 'I am feeling happy!'. Soon, other computer users came up with more variations using a range of characters, some of which are shown at right.

:-(	I am sad
:-O	I am surprised
:-D	I am laughing
;-)	I am winking
8-)	I am wide-eyed or I am wearing glasses
:-&	I am tongue-tied
>-(	I am angry
:-C	I don't believe it!
%-)	I've been staring at the screen too long!

Get more from email

Electronic mail is one of the great features of the Internet and you can do more with it than just send and receive messages. Here we show you what an extraordinary tool email can be.

Exciting possibilities open up when you learn how to attach audio, picture and other files to your email messages.

If you're already connected to the Internet, you have probably started using email in the same way that you would write a letter or send a fax. This one-to-one communication is the most common way of using email and lets you send messages across the world quickly and cheaply. However, although you're using email, you might not be taking advantage of its full range of powerful features.

● **Getting attached**

When you type in an email message and send it to a friend via the Internet, you are using the basic functions of email. One feature of email that you might find useful is to send an attachment with your message.

All you may have to do to attach a file to an email message is click on a paper clip icon, locate the file on your PC and press the Send button.

An attachment is a file that is sent with the message – rather like sending a letter with a package attached to it. The attachment can be any normal file, such as a Word document, Paint image or Excel spreadsheet. You can even send several files at a time. These files are transferred over the Internet to the recipient, who will read your message and open the file(s) attached to it. So, if you have to send reports to the office or just want to send a photograph to relatives in another country, this is a fast, cheap way to move information around the world.

WATCH OUT FOR JUNK

Advertisers can buy lists of email addresses and send unwanted emails promoting a product or service – just like they do through your normal mailbox. These junk-mail messages are intrusive and time consuming. Avoiding junk mail – or spam, as it's known to Internet users – is difficult. Even if there's a note at the bottom of the message about removing yourself from the spammer's list, it's best not to reply to it because it only tells the spammer that you read his message. It's best to ignore all spam.

● Automatic email

So far, we have looked at the ways you can send a message to other people on the Internet (see pages 150–153). If they send a reply, you can read this with your email software. In effect, the system has worked in the same way as the post office delivers a letter. However, millions of people use email to keep up to date with news and features that cover a particular area of interest. This system is called a mailing list and there are tens of thousands of different mailing lists – covering just about every subject and hobby you can imagine.

To subscribe to a mailing list you need to send an email message to the computer that manages the list. Once you have subscribed, you will then receive any new information that is posted to the list. Any of the members on a list can post information that they think might be useful to other members. For example, if you want to learn Spanish, you might want to subscribe to a mailing list covering the Spanish language. The beauty of mailing lists is that once you have subscribed, the information arrives automatically on your computer and you can read it using your usual email software.

Because there are thousands of different mailing lists and they are not usually publicized, you need to use a special database containing all the available lists. There are several of these 'lists of lists' on the Internet and

Getting email without an email program

THE INCREASED availability of the Internet in libraries, Internet cafés, airports, colleges and other locations all over the world makes the possibility of being able to pick up your email from any computer with Internet access look like an extremely good idea. With the Microsoft service Hotmail, you can do just that. A Hotmail account holder simply has to log on to the Hotmail site, then enter his or her user

This Hotmail screen (www.hotmail.com) shows just how simple it can be to log on and collect your email. Simply type in your name, password and click Sign in. Hotmail gives access to email from anywhere in the world.

name and password to be able to pick up any email that is waiting. All the user needs to collect or send email this way is access to a computer with a browser, such as Netscape Navigator or Microsoft Internet Explorer, loaded and running and a connection to the Internet. Hotmail is used by millions of people around the world.

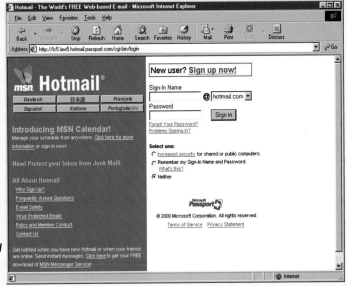

one of the most popular is called Liszt – it's found at www.liszt.com. It contains details of 90,000 mailing lists on the Internet and lets you search through the database lists that cover your areas of interest. Once you have selected a list that sounds suitable, it tells you how to subscribe to it or discover more about the list.

● Subscribing to a list

Subscribing to a mailing list is easy – you send an email with a key phrase (Liszt helps you find this) to the manager of the mailing list, which then adds you to it. Each mailing list has a different key phrase, so read the subscription instructions carefully. When you send your

email asking to subscribe, you'll normally address it to the 'majordomo'. This is a program that reads your email and, if it detects the key phrase, will automatically add you to the list.

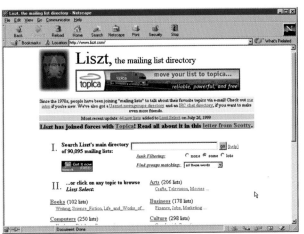

The Liszt site (www.liszt.com) is a comprehensive directory of over 90,000 mailing lists. It works like a search engine as you type in a search term. Always check the nature of the mailing list before you join (see PC Tips).

Adding an attachment to an email message

Email is a great way to send files around the world easily and cheaply. Here's your guide to attaching a photograph to a message – and the method is the same when sending other file types.

1 Launch your email program using the Start button. Here we are using Netscape Messenger, supplied as part of the Netscape Communicator suite and of which the browser Navigator is a part, but other email programs work in a similar way. When Netscape Messenger has loaded, Click on the New Msg button in the toolbar (inset).

2 Clicking on the New Msg button opens a new, blank email document.

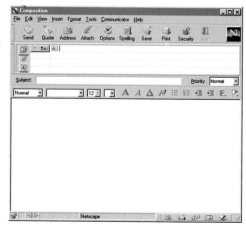

3 Enter the email address in the To: box. In this example we are sending a message to a relative in Australia. Move your cursor to the Subject: box and click to type in a description of the message.

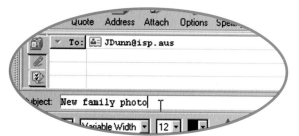

4 Now we're ready to enter the main message. Email is great for a short note like this – updating a relative on the latest family developments. We are going to attach a photograph to the message, so when we've finished typing, we click on the paper-clip Attach button on the toolbar.

5 Hold down the mouse button on the Attach button and then click on File from the drop-down menu that appears. A window opens that says Enter File to attach. We're looking for a photo in the My Pictures folder, which is within the My Documents folder. Double-click on the My Pictures folder to open it and then double-click on the photo you want.

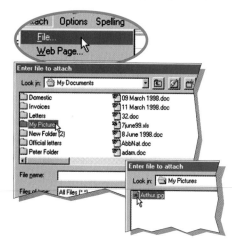

6 Double-clicking on the photo automatically attaches it to your message, which appears as an icon in the panel above the Subject: box. Once you have connected to your Internet service provider, click on the Send button on the toolbar and your message will be sent, complete with the attached photograph.

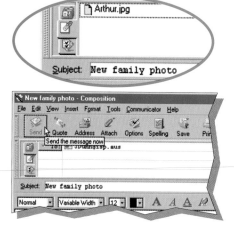

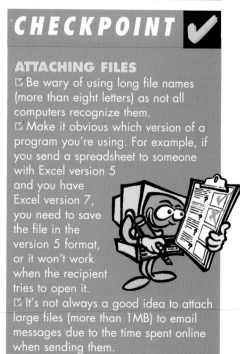

CHECKPOINT ✔

ATTACHING FILES

☑ Be wary of using long file names (more than eight letters) as not all computers recognize them.

☑ Make it obvious which version of a program you're using. For example, if you send a spreadsheet to someone with Excel version 5 and you have Excel version 7, you need to save the file in the version 5 format, or it won't work when the recipient tries to open it.

☑ It's not always a good idea to attach large files (more than 1MB) to email messages due to the time spent online when sending them.

Keep your email address forever

You might want to change to a faster or more reliable ISP, but you'll need to tell everyone your email address has changed. Here we show you how to register with Bigfoot to receive a free email address that you can keep as long as you like.

1 Start your Internet browser and connect to the Bigfoot site at www.bigfoot. com. Click on the join bigfoot tab at the top of the page (inset).

2 On the next screen that appears, you have to fill in your name and current email address. Click the Go button to proceed (inset below).

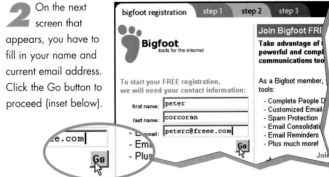

3 You now go to the main registration procedure, where you have to fill in some more information about your location.

Next, you have to select and type in a password, repeating it for confirmation. Choose something that you can remember but that nobody else is likely to guess.

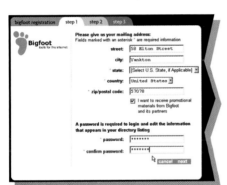

4 The next screen asks for your gender and gives you an option to supply your birthday so you can receive a free horoscope. You can also select one of three levels of privacy – determining whether or not your email address is fully listed. For the time being, accept the default setting; you can always alter this at a later date.

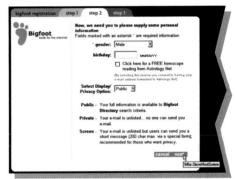

5 On the next screen that appears, either click on stop to halt the procedure or click on continue to go to the next stage where you choose your Bigfoot user name. If you continue, the service will suggest a few alternatives, but you can pick any name you like – as long, of course, as it has not already been taken by someone else. Once you've entered your user name, click the next button.

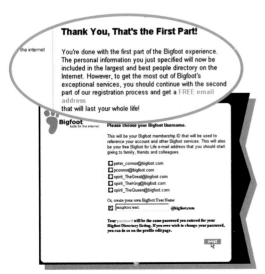

6 The first of a series of three screens that now appears offers you a permanent Web address in much the same way that Bigfoot gives you a permanent email address. The second screen gives you the option to divulge more personal information and the third asks about hobbies and interests. Just click 'next' on the first two of these screens and then Finish on the third, final one to proceed. You will see a screen, warning you that Bigfoot will not tolerate members sending spam (unwanted junk email). Click the 'accept' button to go to the final registration screen, where you will see a message telling you that you are now a Bigfoot For Life member.

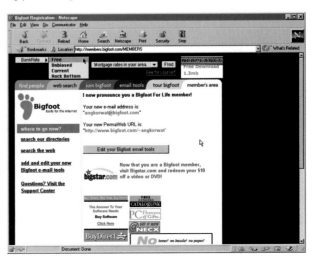

● **Acknowledgments**

Abbreviations; t = top; b = bottom; r = right;
l = left; c = center.
All cartoons are by Chris Bramley

8 De Agostini
11tr De Agostini
12 Dave Jordan/De Agostini
16 Steve Bartholomew/De Agostini
18t Steve Bartholomew/De Agostini
20br N Lloyd/De Agostini
20tl De Agostini
21tr N Lloyd/De Agostini
22 De Agostini
24 Steve Bartholomew/De Agostini
25tl Image Bank
25b De Agostini
27tl Steve Bartholomew/De Agostini
30 De Agostini
32tr De Agostini
33br De Agostini
34 Dave Jordan/De Agostini
35tr Dave Jordan/De Agostini
36 De Agostini
40 Gettyone Stone
44tr Steve Bartholomew/De Agostini
      (background: Image Bank)
44bl Steve Bartholomew/De Agostini
47 Steve Bartholomew/De Agostini
48 De Agostini
51l Dave Jordan/De Agostini
52 De Agostini
54 Steve Bartholomew/De Agostini
56 De Agostini

58-59 De Agostini
60b Gettyone Stone
61b Steve Bartholomew/De Agostini
62 De Agostini
64 Steve Bartholomew/De Agostini
66 De Agostini
68 De Agostini
70t Steve Bartholomew/De Agostini
72 De Agostini
74br Steve Bartholomew/De Agostini
76 De Agostini
78 Gettyone Stone
80 De Agostini
82 Steve Bartholomew/De Agostini
83tr Steve Bartholomew/De Agostini
84-85 De Agostini
88 De Agostini
89-90 (all) De Agostini
91 De Agostini
92 Dave Jordan/De Agostini
93t Gettyone Stone
93c Steve Bartholomew/De Agostini
93b Science & Society Picture Library,
      London
94 Steve Bartholomew/De Agostini
95 Steve Bartholomew/De Agostini
96 De Agostini
98 (all) Steve Bartholomew/De Agostini
99-101 De Agostini
103 De Agostini
106 De Agostini
108l Bridgeman Art Library, London
108tr, cr & br Telegraph Colour Library

108bc De Agostini
110 De Agostini
112 Steve Bartholomew/De Agostini
114t D. Jordan/De Agostini
114b De Agostini
115-117 De Agostini
118 De Agostini
120-123 De Agostini
124 Allsport
126 Image Bank
130tl & cr Gettyone Stone
130tc TRIP
130c De Agostini
134t Dave Jordan/De Agostini
134br TRIP
136 Robotics
138t Steve Bartholomew/De Agostini
138b Global Village
139t Image Bank
139c Global Village
140 Steve Bartholomew/De Agostini
142tr, cr Fortean Picture Library
142b Kobal Collection
143 De Agostini
144br Fortean Picture Library
145 De Agostini
150t Image Bank
150b De Agostini
151t Image Bank
153 Image Bank
154 De Agostini (background NASA)